KV-063-257

Ronnie Knox Mawer grew up in Wrexham, North Wales. During the Second World War he served in the Royal Horse Artillery and then read law at Emmanuel College, Cambridge. After being called to the Bar, he served with HM Overseas Judiciary until 1970. He has now retired from the Bench and devotes his time to writing. His many short stories have been published in such magazines as *Punch*, *Cornhill Magazine* and *Argosy*, and his book *Tales from a Palm Court*, a hilarious account of his experiences as a judge in the Middle East and South Seas, was published in 1986. He and his wife June, a regular broadcaster with the BBC and a published writer, divide their time between Wales and London. They have a son and daughter.

By the same author

TALES FROM A PALM COURT

RONNIE KNOX MAWER

Tales of a Man Called Father

Futura

A Futura Book

Copyright © 1989 by Ronnie Knox Mawer

The lines from the songs 'On the Sunny Side of the Street'
by Dorothy Fields and 'Toodle-oo' by Lombardo and Loeb
are reproduced by permission of EMI Music Publishing Ltd

The line from the song 'Run, Rabbit, Run' is quoted by
permission of Campbell and Noel Gay

First published in Great Britain in 1989 by Souvenir Press
Ltd

This edition published by Futura Publications in 1990

All rights reserved.
No part of this publication may be reproduced,
stored in a retrieval system, or transmitted, in any
form or by any means without the prior
permission in writing of the publisher, nor be
otherwise circulated in any form of binding or
cover other than that in which it is published and
without a similar condition including this
condition being imposed on the subsequent
purchaser.

ISBN 0 7088 4763 3

Reproduced, printed and bound in Great Britain by
BPCC Hazell Books
Aylesbury, Bucks, England
Member of BPCC Ltd.

Futura Publications
A Division of
Macdonald & Co (Publishers) Ltd
Orbit House
1 New Fetter Lane
London EC4A 1AR
A member of Maxwell Macmillan Pergamon Publishing Corporation

CONTENTS

CHAPTER 1

HOME MOVIES

It was somehow typical of Father that his behaviour when departing from this world was thoroughly uncooperative. Just as his huge coffin was being lowered into the grave at Wrexham Cemetery, the sling broke. There was an awkward pause in the ceremony. Amongst the undertaker's men it was debated whether a lever was necessary to rectify the situation. I was reminded of one of Father's more cryptic sayings.

'Give me a lever long enough and strong enough,' he used to declare, quoting Archimedes, 'and I will move the world.'

A lever was found sufficient to move Father.

The waste of time involved would not have met with his approval. Nor would the lack of efficiency on the part of Mr Harrison the undertaker. In the end, however, the blame as usual would have rested with me.

'If there's a decision to be made you can be sure he takes the wrong one — even over my funeral.' I could almost hear Father's high-pitched querulous voice again.

'What do you expect when he goes to Harrison instead of Hoskyn Maggs?' Mr Maggs was the other Wrexham undertaker and, as I should have remembered, a Mason. Father's dedication to the Secret Brotherhood had been the central pillar of his life. Even his obituary in the *Wrexham Leader* carried the banner headline DEATH OF PROMINENT FREEMASON. Strategically placed between the advertisement for Williams delicious pork pies and Border ales, the wine of Wales, was Father's photograph — all six foot and eighteen stone of him, in a business suit of dreadnought grey. Above the starched wing collar, and apothecaries' guild tie (purple measuring scales on a black background), Father glared out at the world through steel-rimmed spectacles, as he had done for fifty years over the counter of his chemist shop.

His background, however, was far from pharmaceutical. He came of a long hard line of North Sea shipmasters. Each of them, — my grandfather Captain Robert, my great grandfather Captain George, my great great grandfather Captain John, my great great great grandfather Captain William — successfully survived life on the ocean waves through a combination of tyrannical energy and fanatical discipline. Father continued the tradition, completely forgetting that he was safely on dry land.

The land in question was North Wales, where Father set up business in High Street, Wrexham. There he met my mother. At nineteen, she was the eldest of six orphaned children. On his marriage Father pressganged the entire family into his service until the boys were old enough to make their escape to America. Fortunately Mother soon provided Father with a replacement crew, of whom I was number four.

The early years of my life seem to me now like one of those home movies that were so popular in the 1930's, a jerky series of episodes and pictures with no particular chronology. Oddly enough Father himself was the first person in Wrexham to use one of the hand operated movie cameras. That was a demonstration model of enormous weight from his chemist shop, which he was trying to sell. Unfortunately the only film he made — of the 1929 hospital carnival — was entirely out of focus. So the machine went back to the makers with a sharp note of complaint.

Luckily I had my own cinematograph in my head, recording images of our family life that are with me still.

What makes them unforgettable is the extraordinary figure who plays the central role. Even when not directly in the picture, his gigantic shadow is forever thrown across the screen, as he looms behind the camera, dragooning us all into action.

That figure is Father, and this is his film.

CHAPTER 2

RESTHAVEN

The setting for most of the scenes was our gaunt Victorian villa in Grosvenor Road, Wrexham. Father named it Resthaven — or rather Rest Haven as he pronounced it — although rest was not something altogether associated with iron bedsteads, acres of cold linoleum, and alarm clocks permanently set at six am. Only the woodworm in the beams could have regarded the place as a haven. Even so, no humour was intended in the name.

'I've no room for comedians in this house,' he observed.

Visitors — of whom there were naturally few — first encountered the entrance hall, a gloomy cavern panelled with the remnants of the Ebenezer Chapel in Poyser Street, and hung with sombre biblical prints — Lazarus Rising from the Dead, The Woman taken in Adultery, Cain in the Act of Slaying Abel.

Through the heavily curtained door of the dining-room Father's voice would be heard, frequently raised in complaint.

'How many times does that boy have to be told to sit up straight?

'Is he determined to grow up a hunchback?

'Where is my soup spoon?

'When will Constance Mary learn to cut the bread straight?

'Sheer wastefulness upon Evelyn's part leaving all that fat.'

The state of the condiments, which had to be arranged

about his bottle of ginger beer like Stonehenge, attracted particular condemnation.

'This mustard, Clara. A very poor effort. She'll have to go.'

He was referring to Edith, our maid.

While Edith assisted the rest of us to clear the long narrow mahogany table, used for lunch and supper, Father removed himself to the fireplace. His fireside chair, in the dining-room, was the central landmark of the house. Its design was spartan and strange. When pressure was applied by the occupant, the hard leather seat slid back between enormous arms of polished oak into a semi-reclining position. This enabled Father to stretch out his legs, while reading the evening paper, thereby blocking the fire from the rest of the family. With the paper carefully folded and laid aside, he resumed the upright position. In a trice, the chair had been transformed into a kind of pulpit from which he delivered a round of homilies to whoever happened to be present. There was an ecclesiastical ring to the monotonous rise and fall of his voice. It was pitched in a minor key. A stranger passing the gate might have thought he was catching the distant sound of plainsong.

'Never put off to the morrow what can be done today . . .

'Only a poor workman quarrels with his tools . . .

'Neither a borrower nor a lender be . . .

'The devil makes work for idle hands . . .

'An early bird catches the worm . . .

'Elbow grease is the best polish . . .

'Quick's the word, sharp's the action, so less talk more speed . . .'

Behind the chair hung a picture that epitomised his whole outlook on life, an engraving of the Victorian painting by Ford Maddox Brown entitled WORK. It was a study of a London highway where street works were in progress. In the centre of the canvas was a navvy, deep in rubble with pick and spade. Above him, at pavement level was a well-dressed gentleman in a top hat calmly overseeing the operation.

'Why', Father would ask, 'is that labouring man so obviously content?'

None of us children was given time to suggest an answer.

'Because,' Father proceeded, 'since infancy he has been taught to work.'

On one occasion my second sister Constance Mary ventured to query the function of the top-hatted onlooker.

'He has brains,' was Father's reply, 'he is the provider of work.'

I understood the message from an early age. Father was brainy. Therefore all he had to do was supervise the rest of us while we 'worked'.

To be perfectly fair to Father, I appreciated that he did in fact earn a living with his brains. Eventually I would be expected to do the same, but at this elementary stage of my evolution I must be taught to work with my hands. And the sooner the better.

From the age of five, I was taught to lace up Father's boots. This was done according to an arcane ritual that only Father understood. It took place in front of the fire in the breakfast room before he proceeded to the table.

The boots were standing in front of the fire, ready for me by the fender — to my infant gaze, two huge black leather containers gleaming from Edith's spit and polish. Father's slippers were removed in silence. He then extended his grey woollen feet over a small wooden stool, while Mother levered the boots into place with a brass shoe-horn. My task was to operate the laces. Each leather thong had to be threaded from the bottom hole as far as number five, in horizontal bands. Thereafter I had to change to a criss-cross action, tightening up as I went, on either side. The crucial test was to have an equal length of lace emerging from each top hook. Next came the execution of a single knot, the encircling of the ankle, and finally the making of what Father called a looped nautical. If by mistake I ended in front with a mock-reefer, another of Father's terms, this could only be prized open with the prong of the toasting fork. This was kept on top of the coal scuttle expressly for this emergency. It was certainly not used for hot buttered toast.

Hot buttered toast was an unnecessary luxury, like carpets, of which there was only one, throughout the entire house. That was in the drawing-room.

Father could never come to terms with the drawing-room carpet, a family heirloom, although he did draw some comfort from the fact that it was badly faded and threadbare. By contrast, he held the piano, another heirloom, in high esteem. This was because immense physical effort was required to get any sound out of it. However strongly the keys were pressed down, there only emerged a strange muffled sound, as though someone were playing a barrel organ in outer space. No funeral march could be more depressing than a tune — any tune — played upon that piano.

At times, Father invited the organist from St Mark's Church, Mr Trevor Hughes, to play excerpts from Gilbert and Sullivan upon the instrument. I'm afraid the ordeal drove the skeletal Mr Hughes to an early grave.

The faint sound of Mr Hughes at the keyboard could just be heard in the adjoining room, known as the study. Unfortunately it was not possible for any use to be made of the study because grandfather's desk occupied it, and there was no room for anything or anybody else. The lower section of the desk, a massive slab of mahogany, contained a single gigantic drawer of such enormous weight that two strong men could barely open it. The rest of the bureau was made up of innumerably tiny containers, ornamented with mother-of-pearl knobs, too small for practical use.

Next to the study was the tattered green baize door leading into the kitchen. From a wooden rack over the range, hung Father's long underpants casting a steamy blight over life below stairs. Strictly speaking it was only the back kitchen that was below stairs, or at least below the turn in the stairs which led to the strangely sited water-closet.

This architectural eccentricity was the cause of considerable agitation. Father had a rule which on the face of it appeared decorous and uncomplicated. No person must acknowledge, even by a whisper, that he or she was in occupation of this facility. Unfortunately it was Father's practice to lock himself in there for what seemed hours upon end. When Father's presence was sought, in the carving chair, he would remain silent despite all efforts to discover his whereabouts. Because the WC was positioned in such an out-of-the-way spot nobody would have seen Father enter. And to turn the door handle, however discreetly, to discover whether it was locked would have been regarded by him as an act of the grossest indecency. False reports would trickle in from Percy, Edith's husband, our part-time gardener.

'I saw Mr Knox Mawer leaving the front gate,' he insisted.

'He must have gone back to the shop then,' Mother would say. 'We'd better start supper and Edith can keep his plate hot.'

This we would do. Invariably, halfway through the meal, the dining-room door would be flung open and Father would appear, apoplectic with fury, like the demon in a pantomime.

'Who gave permission for you to start off without me?' he demanded.

'Well, George, we thought . . .'

'Passive resistance, that's what I'm up against in this house, passive resistance.'

There was no resistance, passive or otherwise, when Father used the room immediately above the water-closet — the bathroom. This occupied a considerable area and was even colder than the drawing-room. We were all upstairs by the time Father went in for total immersion, although in my case, because I was afraid of the dark, my bedroom door was left open. The strains of Carol Gibbons and his band — broadcasting direct from the Savoy Hotel — drifted up the landing. Suddenly, GOODNIGHT SWEETHEART I'LL SEE YOU IN THE MORNING was switched off, heralding Father's approach. He paused to adjust the minute hand on the grandfather clock, occasionally winding up the heavy weights inside. There was a sinister interval of five seconds between the tick and the tock, which I associated with Father's slow ascent to the bathroom.

His habit, of taking a bath at an extraordinarily late hour, caused the gravest domestic inconvenience. The kitchen fire had to be stoked into the early hours to ensure that the boiler in the range was hot. The unspoken command to the two unfortunate crew members, so to speak — Mother and Edith — still toiling below, was FULL STEAM AHEAD.

And steam there certainly was. From my pillow I would watch in awed silence — for I was not supposed to be awake — the scene outside. The bathroom door was open with the hot water running into the bath which was surrounded by a great deal of bleached wood. Clouds of steam would billow out into which he would disappear, armed with a jar of anti-rheumatic salts concocted in his dispensary. It was an awesome business. As though the Royal Scot was being prepared, on Euston Station, for a record run to Inverness.

Once Father had launched himself into the water, a

stream of complaints issued through the cracks in the bathroom door.

'Who's been using my body sponge without permission?' 'What has happened to the nail brush?' 'Where are the clean towels?'

Father had a long-handled brush to scrub his back. The operation led to his losing the soap in the foamy depths about him. The wallowing noises ceased and he called angrily out to Mother.

'Am I expected to manage in here with a single bar of soap?'

'There are two extra tablets on the wash basin, dear,' Mother would assure him, 'Coal Tar, George, your favourite sort.'

The heat of the bath had led to a rise in Father's blood pressure. But there was another reason for the particularly horrendous eruption in the bathroom.

Even Father could not fail to notice the impoverished condition of the bath. The enamel had disappeared entirely from the bottom leaving the surface black and cratered like the moon. As he lay uncomfortably there, Father reflected upon his lot. By intellect he deserved to be a professor of chemistry. Why had the improvidence of grandfather Captain Robert made this aspiration unrealistic? When he had married Mother he had saddled himself with a ready-made family. What a disastrous mistake that had been! The addition of us four children had simply added to his responsibilities. What hope had he ever had of breaking out from the tedious drudgery of the shop?

Like the soap bubbles around him, Father's inner frustrations floated to the surface. And the very house itself seemed to echo his grudge against the world. From the decaying rafters of Resthaven to the grim cellar, pipes hissed and clanked their complaints. The cistern boiled and gurgled in the vilest of tempers.

Not until the early hours did the tremors from the angry volcano begin to subside. Clutching a large white towel Father retreated at last to his bedroom. Gradually the sound of running water ceased, as the ballcocks slowly did their job. Mount Etna had subsided at last. Encouraged by a medicinal tot of gin, from the bottle kept under the bed, Father slept.

CHAPTER 3

CHILDREN OF THE CRAFT

The bathroom ritual took place three times a week, on the night before those gatherings which were the ruling passion of his life — the brotherhood of freemasons.

It was Aunty Carrie who cautioned me against the freemasons.

'When you grow up,' she warned, 'don't have nothing to do with them. They'll blacken your dickey!'

Aunty Carrie — as I was allowed to call her — was the plump and elderly spinster who helped with the washing on Mondays.

'Not a word, mind,' she said, spotting Father's grey trilby and the glint of his steel spectacles outside the kitchen window.

'He's got another of his Lodges tonight.'

She took a heavy flat-iron off the hob and brought it thudding down upon another of Father's freshly starched evening shirts. A curious detail in this operation — with Father's comfort in mind — was that the long tail must be unstarched.

'He gets through three of these shirts in one week's Lodges,' she complained.

Mother was busy with another flat-iron on Father's wing collar, size eighteen.

'Did you hear him shaving this morning, Mrs Mawer?' Aunty Carrie went on.

Mother folded a starched white tie and waistcoat, also for the Lodge.

'I don't know what you mean, Miss Rogers,' she pretended.

Aunty Carrie was referring to the ceremonial responses and incantations which Father always rehearsed when operating his cut-throat razor.

'Them mad things he shouts out, Mrs Mawer, about being blindfolded and having tongues pulled out.' Aunty Carrie spat scornfully on the iron to test the heat. Her thudding was resumed.

There were other clues to this secret activity of Father's. On days when his memory let him down he would emerge from his ablutions with several pieces of sticking plaster in the shaving area of his moonlike countenance.

Alongside his chair in the dining-room, on the table half hidden by his latest copy of *The Chemist and Druggist*, was a small black book, sinisterly untitled. At the end of the meal, Father studied its pages, while dipping into his preserved ginger. Occasionally a large tear would roll down his cheek. At first, I associated this unfamiliar display of emotion with the secrets of the black book, until I discovered for myself the fierceness of Father's favourite flavour.

Upon a small table by the wireless set — a pseudo-gothic monument in three tiers — stood Father's unsmiling photograph in Masonic regalia. What he was wearing was never explained to me. About his ample waist he wore what looked like one of Aunty Carrie's tea-time aprons. Except that it was hung with what I thought were horse brasses. As though to complement the equestrian image, Father seemed to be wearing a large halter around his neck.

A slim Masonic suitcase, stamped with all of Father's four initials, was kept locked underneath what he called the chamber cabinet, at the side of his bed. The case accompanied Father everywhere. Even on holiday.

My earliest recollection is of a hot afternoon in Rhyl.

We were paddling in the sea there, my sisters and I. Father was supervising, encouraging us to inhale the salt spray to improve the sinuses. I had no idea what these were.

To my embarrassment, what made him look different from other fathers engaged in the same duty was the dinner jacket he was wearing: along with a starched front, wing collar, and white tie. The dinner jacket had seen better days. No doubt the other holidaymakers assumed him to be an off-duty head waiter, from the other side of the promenade.

The truth was that Father had dressed in good time — four hours to be precise — for the Rhyl Lodge that evening.

'Clara! Clara!' he called. There was no reply.

'Where is your mother?'

Unfortunately, Mother had left his deck-chair unguarded, for a brief call of nature. The beach attendant had removed, to the Lost Property Office, the Masonic case stored by Father under the chair.

'Provincial Grand Rank, Clara!' he thundered, when she reappeared, 'have you any conception what that particular regalia costs?'

After a terrible fuss, the case was retrieved, just as a large black Austin Six drew up on Marine Parade.

'Very kind of you to collect me, Brother Isaac,' Father called, hurrying across the pebbles.

Mother explained to me that Mr Isaac Jones was the biggest taxi proprietor in North Wales. His Austin Six was fitted with special fold-up seats for smaller passengers. I could never imagine Father setting off for a Masonic Lodge in anything but solemn black transport.

Masonry dominated not only Father's life, but mine. All too soon I began to see the point of his question 'What does his father do?', whenever I mentioned a new friend at school. The object was to discover whether the father was a Mason. If so, there was a chance that the friend might be invited home. I was rarely lucky. Few of the fathers of my friends were Masons.

The result was that our children's parties were confined to visiting, and reciprocating the visit of, the family of Worshipful Brother A. J. Rathwell, Father's opposite number in the Masonic craft.

A.J., a small, dynamic man, was a successful Wrexham builder. Mrs A.J. was bright and cheerful. They owned a new home — Sunny Ridge in Acton Drive, a sharp contrast to our gaunt Victorian villa.

We children were dazzled by the mock Elizabethan gables and neo-Jacobean windows of Sunny Ridge, with its wall to wall carpeting throughout. The Rathwells even had a radiogram. Their children's party was an invariable success. The Rathwell twins, Donald and Muriel, were both spoilt. Muriel was positively odious. However the excitement of expensive toys — Hornby train, Dinky car set, dolls' house, plus the gargantuan feast, proved irresistible.

What made our return party so disastrous was not so much the absence of lavish toys; plain jellies and seed cake constituted festive fare in Resthaven. It was Father's insistence upon providing his own version of entertainment. This came at the end of tea.

'Now that you've all finished,' he announced, 'you can answer the general knowledge quiz I have set for you.'

On one memorable occasion Muriel insisted that we played Happy Families instead. I found the cards.

'Sheer vandalism!' Father complained upon sorting them out.

The Happy Families cards were a present from Aunty Carrie which I had improved with a spot of inking-in. Mr Bun the Baker, Mr Lamb the Butcher and Mr Green the Grocer were wearing new steel-rimmed spectacles, wing collars, and severe frowns.

In his striped apron, rolled-up sleeves, and straw hat, Mr Lamb did not look particularly like Father — nor for that matter did Messrs Bun and Green. But the implication was clear.

There had not been much jollity while the jellies and seed cake were going down. Now there was dead silence.

'Is there any more cake?' Donald asked.

'You've had three pieces, Donald,' Mother said, 'I'm afraid you've finished it off.'

I tried to get Radio Luxembourg for Muriel on our wireless set.

Unfortunately the wet battery was too feeble to pick up anything except the national programme.

'Can we go home now?' Muriel asked her parents. 'Even if we've missed the Ovalteenies, we can still hear "Appointment with Death".'

I was not sorry to see them go.

Apart from Worshipful Brother A. J. Rathwell, I remember one other Masonic visitor to Resthaven, threatened rather than actual.

'I've offered to put up Crossley Dennison, Clara,' Father announced at supper time.

It emerged that Crossley Dennison was an important Grand Lodge official from London, attending the Square and Compass Lodge in Wrexham.

'I've told him he can have the guest bedroom,'

We had no guest bedroom.

Father was referring to the box room. With the breakdown in the Disarmament Conference, Father had been 'looking ahead', and the box room was full of emergency hospital supplies — oxygen tents, bed-pans, operating tables, rolls of surgical gauze, orthopaedic supports and a mountain of suppositories.

Mother was busily moving the orthopaedic supports into the laundry cupboard when Father reported that Mr

Dennison had decided to put up at the Wynnstay Arms Hotel instead.

'He's come to lecture the Craft upon Business Standards,' Father continued, 'and not before time.'

He spoke with feeling, since I had recently accompanied Father on a significant mission in this regard. Although I myself had not fully appreciated what it was all about.

'Constance Mary,' Father said, at lunch-time during the Whitsun school holiday, 'I want you to do a spot of sign reading this afternoon.'

I was required to accompany my second sister in Father's decrepit Clino.

'Tell him to sit down this instant,' Father snapped.

I suppose Father thought it instructive for me to have to go along. My problem was feeling sick in the back, from the smell of hot leather, petrol, and oil.

'Apart from blocking my rear-view mirror, his dirty knees are a disgrace!'

Connie glanced over her shoulder sympathetically. We had reached the outskirts of Wynnstay Park.

'That notice board, Constance Mary, to your left,' barked Father, 'does it say Bowman's Farm?'

In a huge belted driving coat, Father looked even more frightening than usual.

The notice did say Bowman's Farm, and Father shuddered to a halt alongside the hay-barn.

'Why it's Worshipful Brother Knox Mawer' exclaimed a jolly red-faced man emerging with a pitch-fork.

'Well, Brother Bowman,' Father answered, 'I've come about this broody hen you sold me. It's no good at all,'

'What's the matter with it?'

'Well for one thing, it's dead,' Father said, tossing the unfortunate creature at Mr Bowman's feet.

Without waiting for a reply, Father ordered us back into the Clino and reversed rapidly up the track.

'I had expected better standards from a member of the Wynnstay Lodge,' was all he said as he drove us home.

'Now you can both get on with your homework. And make sure it's up to standard.'

Not even the offspring of Masons, — known as Children of the Craft, — were exempt from standards. As far as Father was concerned, this meant ten out of ten for every piece of homework completed.

I consulted Aunty Carrie over a question from my history teacher about the grandchildren of Queen Victoria. She was an authority on the Royal Family, for whom she had the warmest enthusiasm.

'Except for the Duke of Clarence,' she warned.

'What was the matter with him, Aunty Carrie?'

'He was one of them,' she said darkly.

'You don't mean . . .' I blushed. 'Surely they wouldn't.'

'They're all tarred with the same brush,' she interrupted grimly, a strikingly apt phrase, it struck me at the time.

'Just you wait and see.'

CHAPTER 4

BODY AND SOUL

It was because I was thought to have a weak chest that Monsignor O'Reilly came into the picture. His Roman Catholic Convent school was only a few doors away from Resthaven, and ideally sited, it seemed to the Monsignor, for the reception of a child in frail health. His visit to make the suggestion to Father was largely a Christian gesture — coupled perhaps with the thought of an extra hundred pounds in fees.

'You'd better take a seat,' Edith said, sensing trouble, 'I'll tell Mr Mawer you've come.'

The prelate was a newcomer to the district. Otherwise he would have kept well clear of Father, with or without his prospectus. The Pope himself would have enjoyed a happier time at the hands of Oliver Cromwell.

'No child of mine will be attending a Roman Catholic school, I can promise you that.' Father's voice was like thunder as the mistaken cleric retreated down the front doorsteps repeating 'pax Domini, pax Domini'. At least he escaped the fate of an earlier predecessor, the Blessed Richard Gwynn, who had rashly attempted the conversion of Protestant Wrexham and was martyred for his cause on the neighbouring market square in 1584.

'The child will have to go to Ivy Toft,' Father decided, when the priest had gone, 'for the time being at least.'

At first I thought Ivy Toft was some lady teacher who had happened to win Father's approval, the wife perhaps of a Masonic neighbour. As it turned out, it was the name of a seedy establishment on the corner of Grosvenor Road, shrouded in evergreens and run by Miss Weatherby, daughter of the founder, a vague and forgetful lady with a bun.

At the time of my enrolment in her school — 1929 — Father's bulk-buying was targeted at the Army and Navy Surplus Stores in Queen Street. So I arrived at Miss Weatherby's door, parcelled up in an immense dark blue muffler (heavy duty, naval ratings for the use of) criss-crossed over the front of my mackintosh and knotted at the back in a system devised by Father 'to keep out the elements'. It was topped by a yellow sou'wester — the Dartmouth Junior. However Miss Weatherby did not appear to notice. In fact she seemed not to notice me at all during the next eighteen months.

'Is he learning anything whatsoever there, Clara?' Father wanted to know. He decided to give me an elementary test. The BBC announcer had just told us that Malcolm Campbell had broken the land-speed record in his racing car Bluebird.

'Write the name down for me,' Father said.

BLEW BERD, I wrote, after much labour with pencil and rubber.

As always, Father moved rapidly. Within a week I was removed from Ivy Toft, pronounced fit, and despatched to walk four miles each day to Acton Park Council School. Here Father relentlessly monitored my progress. Within six months I was required, at his command, to rattle off the names of the kings and queens of England since 1066, to add up like a midget computer, and to make deadly sure in spelling that the i came before e excepting after c.

My lightning posting to Acton was just one more example of the alacrity of Father's decisions as far as I was concerned. A few coughs in Father's presence led instantly to my having tonsils out. An occasional sneeze led to the brisk removal of my adenoids. It was the same with my first teeth. At Father's hands they were down like ninepins.

With my doctors and dentists, Father imposed only one condition — that they were members of the Craft.

As to my teeth, my position was especially perilous, because Resthaven was surrounded by dentists. Dental Surgeon Brother Esmor Hooson, for instance, practised from the house immediately opposite our dining-room, with his chair in the bay window. As I sat eating my prunes I was obliged to watch his macabre acrobatics with the drill, before going across for my turn.

Looking back, it strikes me that Father had a tendency to use me for the furtherance of trade.

'That stethoscope you're using on him, Doctor Glynn,' he would bark, over my wheezes, 'must be about time it was replaced. Rubber looks to be badly perished. Have you seen my new line from Medicraft?'

Or when Doctor Wallace was taking my temperature.

'Marking's quite worn away on your thermometer, Doctor Wallace. You'll not be getting an accurate reading while you hang on to that.'

There were few requirements which Father could not supply, and he did a particularly lively business in face-masks for the administration of nitrous oxide.

'The boy seems to have another gum-boil,' Father would enthuse to Mr Hooson. 'A whiff of gas, then a quick wrench, eh?'

I have no wish to exaggerate. Father was a conscientious parent, and I still retained sufficient molars with which to get by. But if business could be combined with paternal watchfulness, then so much the better.

On extremely rare occasions, Father himself was laid low.

'No Clara, I do *not* need Dr Wallace. I should know an upper respiratory infection when I've got one.'

He returned to bed where he lay propped up against a hard bolster upon his large lumpy mattress.

'Send Edith upstairs with a bowl of boiling water,' he told Mother, 'and bring a towel.'

Swathed in Mother's white towel, Father scattered a palmful of menthol crystals onto the water, then bent his head over the bowl to inhale the fumes.

'More hot water,' he would gasp, emerging, red-faced from the steam, like an enraged Sheikh of Araby.

Hanging just behind him, was a long cord with a knob on the end. The cord disappeared into the ornate cornice above his head. From there it was connected with an elaborate system of interior wire cable. The cable led to the sixth bell in a row above the kitchen door, which Father constantly rang.

'He'll be wanting me, Mrs Mawer,' Aunty Carrie insisted, with a touch of malice. She would march upstairs with the soup that Mother had taken great pains to prepare.

'Oh, well done, Miss R,' Father would approve. 'Your own special broth! Always the best cure for me.'

There were just two classes in Father's household — the Officer class which was Father, and the Other Ranks, being the rest of us. Bridging the gap was Aunty Carrie who obviously carried an invisible lance corporal's stripe upon her chubby arm.

'Those children are making a lot of noise, Miss R.'

Down marched the Lance Corporal with a list of jobs dictated by Father.

Weed shrubbery
Water cactus — the cactus died from too much water
Scrape up pigeon droppings
Pick up dead leaves
Dig in compost
Feed ducks

Pick up more dead leaves

While my sisters were picking up more leaves, Mother and I peeped in on the patient. He had switched on the wireless extension.

Enid Hitchcock and her Ladies Ensemble, broadcasting live from Torquay, were playing 'Body and Soul', with three violins, two violas, harp and piano. Father was staring out of the window, his cheeks purple, with a glazed expression on his face. It looked to me as though he had overdone the menthol crystals again.

'Would you like one of your blood-pressure pills, George?' Mother suggested. Father shook his head, breathing heavily.

'I'm keeping those for the End,' he declared.

Standing behind Mother, with the rejected glass of water, I heard Father recite his favourite lines of Tennyson.

> And may there be no moaning of the bar
> When I put out to sea.

These gloomy verses by Queen Victoria's poet laureate were contained in a large volume kept by his bedside. This was something I discovered when first attending Acton School.

Miss Edwards, our teacher, had handed out copies of the latest publication by Mr Arthur Mee, the editor of the *Children's Newspaper. Rhyming Fun for the Very Young.*

'Choose any one of the poems you like,' she told us, 'and learn it by heart. You'll each recite what you've chosen to the class tomorrow morning.'

Back home I brought Arthur Mee's Magnus Opus out of my school satchel.

'You'd better come upstairs and let your Father decide,' Mother advised. Father thumbed quickly through the pages.

'A very poor anthology,' he decided. He reached down for Tennyson's Complete Works. 'Let me see now. Pity, Clara, there isn't time for him to get his teeth into *The Death of King Arthur*.' Mother was refilling his hot-water bottle. In a sepulchral whisper — partly due to his sore throat — he read out a chunk of *In Memoriom*.

'A bit too long again, I suppose. Let me see. Ah. Yes. Here we are.'

He had alighted on a shorter poem.

'Entirely suitable,' he decided.

Next morning, Donald Rathwell gave a spirited rendering of *Albert and the Lion*.

'Now it's your turn,' said Miss Edwards brightly.

I stood up.

> 'Break, break, break [I began],
>   On thy cold gray stones, O Sea!
> And I would that my soul could utter
>   The thoughts that arise in me.'

There was an awkward silence.

'Just a wee bit soulful,' said Miss Edwards, but once started, there was no stopping me.

> 'And the stately ships go on
>   To their haven under the hill;
> But O for the touch of a vanish'd hand,
>   And the sound of a voice that is still.'

Rita Williams, a sensitive little girl, began sobbing in the corner.

'That's quite enough, Ronnie,' said Miss Edwards firmly. She turned to the class.

'Time now for our rhyming singsong.'

She leaned towards me.

'And please tell your father that I would prefer you to stick to the school syllabus in future.'

CHAPTER 5

A MONTH OF SUNDAYS

'Good Day to you, then, Padre,' said Father.

'And — er — to you too, Mr Knox Mawer,' replied the Reverend Arthur Fowles who'd been a life-long conscientious objector.

Together with the verger, Father and I usually constituted the whole of the early morning congregation at St Mark's Church, a building of stunning ugliness with hard pews and a solitary Victorian monument. This was a marble coffin with a white hand emerging from it. It had been commissioned by Mr John Jones, the Wrexham brewer (of Number Two Grosvenor Road) and showed his sadly lamented daughter making a limp effort to rise from the tomb on Resurrection Day. Father, who enjoyed a healthy interest in death, was particularly fond of the monument. But less fond of the vicar.

'Another hopeless sermon,' he said. I think we were just about out of earshot of Canon Fowles, who was still standing at the entrance to the porch.

To me, the gargoyle immediately above the vicar's head wore a familiar look. It had Father's stony glare. I was confronted by this shortly afterwards when, back at home, he poked his head around the shabby green baize kitchen door.

'The devil makes work for idle hands,' he snapped.

So far as I was concerned I was far from idle. I was struggling to swallow the tablespoonful of Malt n' Oil pushed into my mouth by Aunty Carrie. This was one of Father's edicts, to be complied with daily, twice on Sundays. At the same moment, a vile smell drifted in from the back yard, where my youngest sister was engaged in her Sunday task — brewing up the mash. Father sniffed approvingly.

The mash — for his livestock — consisted of disgusting kitchen scraps heated with bran over an Army field stove. The bran was ordered in bulk, like the gravel for the paths, which was never less than six inches deep and a considerable danger to the very young and the very old.

Father's obsession with Bulk Orders meant that he was frequently at the Surplus Store in Hope Street, snapping up bargains — his words — left over from the Great War. These included a large number of demob trilby hats.

'Get out here and give me a hand,' he told me. 'You'll need one of my hats.'

Father paid great attention to the head — to everybody's head, in fact. During the Depression, people came begging at our door. On one occasion Father sent an entire family away, with every member — even the tiniest of the children — in one of his dark grey trilby hats.

It began to rain. This was Father's moment for one of his rare quips.

'Line up the human chain,' he called from the side door, where he was safely sheltered, while directing operations.

The human chain comprised my three sisters, Aunty Carrie and me. Our job was to hand along buckets of the mash from the back yard to the feeding troughs.

'Bring out the mackintoshes,' came the next command.

From a row of nails, by the cellar steps, hung a line of Father's Army Surplus raincoats. They were all identical in design and colour, a dismal fawn. The sleeves of mine seemed especially long, hanging right over my hands.

I sometimes dream that the whole of my childhood was spent trudging about in the mud, at 26 Grosvenor Road, in that raincoat, totally waterlogged.

'What has the boy done with the planteasy?' came

Father's voice from the other side of the coke shed. The planteasy was a special implement in which Father had invested. It was supposed to make holes in the ground. The name was a gross misrepresentation for which the makers would nowadays be prosecuted under the Trade Description Act.

'In the second greenhouse, Father,' I coughed.

The fumes from the mash had reached the point of combustion when everyone began to choke except Father.

The garden at Resthaven was the normal modest size for a suburban Victorian villa. However Father had divided it into an extraordinary number of rather grandly named sections. There was the Shrubbery — two or three depressed laurel bushes; the Rose Garden, a smallish area like a crossword puzzle with narrow concrete paths terminating in four tiny Rose Arbours, or Rose Harbours, as Father called them. This was not so much a mistake in pronounciation as a subconscious echo of his nautical ancestry.

Adjoining the wall of our neighbours, the Herford Jenkins, was the so-called Orchard. There, in the middle of no more than half a dozen fruit trees, Father had sunk an iron bath, a second-hand specimen that struck me as much superior to our own. This he referred to as the Duck Pond.

Father insisted upon a duck egg for breakfast — a meal always taken alone in the dining-room. The egg had to be supplied by one of his Khaki Campbell Runners. Led by a ferocious goose (Father's Christmas dinner), these incontinent birds gobbled up the mash in a quagmire of mud.

The result was especially unfortunate on Sunday afternoons when the Herford Jenkins family endeavoured to have tea in their summerhouse.

Mr H. J. was a fiery ex-Major — Army Dental Corps.

'Public disgrace!' came his bark from the other side

of the wall. 'Serious health hazard! Intend to notify the Sanitary Inspector!'

Volleys of un-Christian exchanges ricocheted back and to across the frontier of a fortified brick wall.

Father particularly objected to Major Herford Jenkins' yellow waistcoat.

'Why does the fellow have to dress like a canary?' he demanded loudly. 'Can you tell me that, Clara?'

'And why does he have to take all the light off my sweet-peas with that ridiculous shed he calls a summerhouse?'

'Remind me to get some more barbed wire and broken glass put up on my side. I notice I'm losing a great deal of fruit. What trust can one put in one's neighbours these days? I ask you.'

These rhetorical questions were punctuated by a snap of his secaturs, as he paraded the gooseberry bushes, Father's favourite fruit.

'And all this rubbish about his wife being stung by one of my bees. How can he prove that, eh? Tell me that, Clara.'

Mother maintained a discreet silence during these Sabbath hostilities. Yet, in our militant neighbour's view, the bees, the barbed wire, the broken glass, even the ducks, were nothing like as offensive as Father's racing pigeons.

Scowling down upon the Major's property was a kind of Mad Hatter's castle known as The Lofts. As a boy, Father had been given a tame racing pigeon. He embarked upon the sport later in life without explanation. But on a gigantic scale. The Lofts extended over a considerable area, a shaky construction of wooden cages, cat-walks and ladders. Two grown men were engaged in the enterprise. There was Mr Tombs — who also did some gardening — and Mr Perry, the Loft Manager, both small of stature, in threadbare mufflers and caps. On Sundays they were off duty and I was their deputy.

'Release the fledglings,' Father called up to me, his foot on the bottom rung of one of the ladders. A flock of downy young birds fluttered down onto the cabbage patch.

'Now the San Sebastians.'

The San Sebastians were pedigree cocks in training for the main race of the season — a homing flight from San Sebastian in Spain.

'Coo-coo-coooooooo.' Father used what he fancied to be a sweetly wooing tone while his armada described a token circle or two in the sky. Then he took to shaking a large bowl of corn. The pigeons took no notice whatsoever of these enticements to return. Instead they settled on the roof of Major Herford Jenkins.

In a few moments a loud cry of rage emerged from one of the upper windows.

'Those damn birds are fouling my skylights again.'

'And what about those crows of yours?' Father pointed a quivering hand to the nests at the top of the Major's elm tree. 'They've pecked nearly every seed of that grass I planted along the herbaceous borders.'

Fortunately both adversaries were dedicated listeners to the national news. Six o'clock meant a brief armistice as they retreated indoors to their respective wireless sets, summoned by the BBC call-sign of the Daventry Bells.

As with the League of Nations, no cessation of hostilities lasted for long.

CHAPTER 6

COLD COMFORT

Father's remedy for my frequent bad colds during winter was invariably the same.

'I'll take him for a brisk walk through the Rhosddu Road Burial Ground, Clara,' he would say.

With a throbbing head and streaming nose I was required to follow him to this melancholy site. Upon most occasions there was a harsh wind blowing from the east. Looking back, it was surprising that I did not develop bronchitis, let alone pneumonia, which in those days was usually fatal. It would be wrong however to assume that Father had in mind a timely reminder of mortality. The chief purpose of the expedition was all the invigorating climbing involved, because the hills were steep upon that side of town.

'Much better than lying about in a stuffy bedroom,' he would call back to me, while I crunched my way through another throat lozenge — the black pebbled variety (surplus to stock), smelling of iodine and tar.

'None of that syrupy rubbish,' he insisted.

Although out of breath, I was always anxious not to get too far behind, especially when we approached the actual entrance. This was a Victorian archway of Gothic design. The grey stones had become blackened, due to the Great Western railway cutting which ran below. Looking up through the swirling mist I could just pick out the date — 1849, which struck me as Old Testament time. To the left of the central arch was the former keeper's house. The sole tenants were bats and an occasional owl. Much more sinister, and the most pressing reason why I did not want to be left behind, was the building to the right of the arch. This had no windows, simply an enormous pair of double doors with a cross above them.

'This was where the body was kept while the grave was being dug,' Father explained. 'Of course the hearses were horse-drawn in those days, and the driver and his mate needed very wide double doors to get the coffins in and out.'

To my mind the worst thing about those doors was the fact that they seemed to be permanently closed. What was behind them? The black paint was peeling off and sometimes the wood would creak as I hurried past.

'How long would they have to stay in there?' I quavered.

'It all depended upon the gravedigger.'

What did he mean? I asked myself, managing to catch him up again.

'If he was an energetic digger, a good worker (Father's favourite expression) — about four hours. Assuming the plot was already occupied he wouldn't have far to dig, would he?'

'Wouldn't he?' I enquired desperately. In spite of myself the subject held a dreadful fascination.

'What if he dug too far?'

'His spade would come upon the coffin underneath. Or what remained of it.'

Mesmerised, like a rabbit, I had to go on.

'What if the weather was bad?'

'If the ground was frozen, who knows!'

I had a nightmare vision of the lazy gravedigger, one whose activities had been held up indefinitely by a heavy fall of snow. Perhaps that was exactly what had happened just before the cemetery had been finally closed. I glanced over my shoulder. What if there was still somebody waiting to be buried behind those double doors in the stone mortuary without any windows?

Father was striding purposefully ahead of me again. I overtook him on the track overgrown with dandelions which ran straight through the centre of the Ground. There were so many holes in it that it was impossible to keep my eyes closed for more than three or four steps at a time. Inevitably, when trying to do just this, I blundered onto the verge and was felled by the notice board DOGS NOT ALLOWED.

I looked up to discover the finger of a crumbling angel above my nose. COME UNTO ME ALL YE THAT ARE WEARY AND SORE AFFLICTED, I read on the stone underneath. At that moment I rather wished I could.

'Damn fool,' I heard Father explode. 'Blind as a bat.'

Another horrid picture flashed through my mind. Bats! I scrambled to my feet and hastened onwards. On either side, the dear departed were commemorated in every style of monument.

We were now approaching the grand climax of our expedition — the family plots of Mother's ancestors at the top.

'Poor workmanship,' Father said, prodding with his umbrella at a piece of granite where the lead lettering had fallen away. 'False economy.' O DE TH W ERE IS THY TING, it said. I did not like to ask what it meant.

'Look at these appalling weeds.' Father kicked a clump of daisies with the cap of his polished boot. 'Why they couldn't have settled for a decent load of gravel is beyond me. Shiftless lot.'

We had reached the peak of the hill. The site was dominated by a curious example of the monumental mason's craft — a Doric column broken in two. The top half leaned against the bottom, at an angle of forty-five degrees.

'What happened to this one?' I asked, half expecting another lecture on faulty workmanship.

Father's voice became solemn.

'I'm afraid the design was deliberately chosen. It is meant as a symbol and warning to others.'

The inscription upon the column said

IN LOVING MEMORY OF ERNEST JONES, CLERK, BORN 10th JUNE 1836 DIED 9th JULY 1857.

'He was an uncle on your mother's side,' Father said, 'Came to an early end through Drink.'

Together we studied the lines carved on the ornamental slate underneath.

> HE IS ABSENT FROM THOSE WHO ONCE KNEW HIM
> IT WAS HEAVEN THAT CALLED HIM AWAY
> HE HAS GONE TO THE ONE WHO RECEIVED HIM
> FROM NIGHT TO THE SPLENDOUR OF DAY.

'As long as the opening hours are good,' Father remarked, 'that should suit him to the ground.'

I gasped. Father had made two jokes in one! He was about to make a third. He gestured in the direction of the town beyond the railway line.

'And the family certainly managed to give him his favourite view.'

Dominating the sky-line was the familiar chimney stack of the brewery, flaunting an enormous sign in scarlet paint, BORDER ALES THE WINE OF WALES.

Father resumed his customary sternness.

'I trust you never fail to recall this lesson of a Mis-spent Youth,' he said. 'Your Mother's family blood runs in your veins, which can't be helped now. But it may explain a great deal of certain aspects of your erratic behaviour at home and at school.'

I said nothing. It was time to go home for tea.

Father's exercise in cold therapy was at an end. One more ritual remained. As we left, he would invariably point to the carved letters over the exit side of the gothic arch: TOILERS IN THE FIELD OF THE LORD SHALL RECEIVE THEIR REWARD IN THE HEREAFTER.

This moment was normally passed in silence, but for once I felt emboldened to make an enquiry.

'Does it have to be a field?' I asked.

'A garden will do,' came the reply, as he set off at a quick marching pace in the direction of Resthaven.

CHAPTER 7

THE SORCERER'S APPRENTICE

Not surprisingly, a bank holiday with Father seemed to be different from other people's. Donald and Muriel Rathwell were going with their parents to Rhyl, and I had been invited too. Father said to tell them that unfortunately I had a previous engagement. In fact I had more than one.

The day began with a chorus of discontent from the duck-house, long before dawn. Father had dosed the drake with BUILD U UP (NATURE'S WAY WITH THE OVER FORTIES). This hadn't proved a popular line at the shop. He was adept at putting old stock to new uses.

Sleep was out of the question. Not that it made much difference. Father insisted upon the earliest possible working breakfast for national holidays.

'Business as usual,' was Father's motto. 'Pity it isn't Ramsay Macdonald's' he added, crackling the front page of the *Daily Mail*, 'Gallivanting with the King, at Cowes, when the country's on the scrap-heap.'

'Yes Father,' I said, trotting after him towards the front door.

It took us five minutes to get to the shop, with a ten-second pause at the War Memorial, a life-sized statue of an RWF soldier, collapsed on his banner. I felt a spirit of comradeship as I leaned over the railings, trying to get rid of the stitch in my side.

'Cap off,' Father ordered. He had already made his own bare-headed salute and was striding ahead to the High Street.

'Get those blinds up, quick sharp,' I was told, as he opened the door of the pharmacy.

Coal miners, on their way home from the night shift, were our first customers.

'A ha'penny packet of menthyl crystals for the wife's bad cold.'

I rang up the till, always a source of trouble from its antiquated machinery. The roll stuck immediately. Father's heavy tread advanced from the dispensary behind me.

'Blockhead,' he observed, freeing the lever with a heavy blow. I stood well to one side.

The bank manager was another early caller, enjoying a miserable day off.

'A bottle of your father's Special K 138,' he said hoarsely.

Mr Harrison seemed to have chronic laryngitis. I washed out a clean bottle for him in the dispensary sink.

'Hold the funnel straight,' Father said. From the shelf he took down an enormous glass jar containing a dark brown treacly liquid.

'New cork,' he barked.

I had one ready, together with the label.

Father added a considerable amount of chloroform to the prescription for Mr Harrison, who seemed to be virtually addicted to the mixture.

'He has to have it strong,' Father observed, 'otherwise he asks for his money back.'

He took the K 138 out to the drug counter.

'I suppose you've been up at the golf links again,' Father said sternly. 'Catching your death of cold. I don't know why you don't keep away from the place.'

The golf links, a popular source of relaxation and pleasure for Wrexham's haut-bourgeoisie, attracted Father's particular censure. I think it was the plus-fours he disliked, much favoured by Major Herford Jenkins. 'You'll not catch Farmer Hartley wasting his time at any golf club,' Father observed, when the bank manager had gone, and his space at the counter taken over by one of our agricultural clients.

'Check up on the salt-licks for Mr Hartley,' he told me. 'I rather think we've run short.'

'Out of stock, Father,' I confirmed, after my usual struggle with the trap-door leading down to the cellar where these items were normally kept.

At least there were no rats in the cellar; conditions were uncongenial for rats. A diet of carbolic acid and salt-licks did not appeal to them at all. The cellar was lit by a grating in the pavement above. Through the bars I watched a procession of feet go by as the first charabanc of the day, for Rhyl, loaded up just outside.

'Any more passengers for the day trip?' I heard the driver say.

'One down here,' I said to myself, translated for a moment to holiday sands and candy floss.

'What on earth's keeping you down there?', called a furious voice through the trap, 'nip up smartly to the stock room for the chilblain ointment.' 'Can't think for the life of me why Mrs Jones has got chilblains at this time of the year,' I heard him muttering to himself as he returned to the counter.

The stock room was on the third of the four storeys of the shop, a building erected in 1810 — when George the Third was King, as the motto on Father's business paper pointed out.

Up the first flight of iron-tipped stairs was the surgical room, where the local ladies were fitted out with elastic stockings and other private aids to glamour.

From there the narrow steps led to the poisons room. I could never resist the temptation to look into that sinister apartment. No doubt, I remember thinking, Donald Rathwell would return from Rhyl with an account of his visit to the cinema there. Father did not approve of cinemas. Donald habitually described in lurid detail, the latest thriller he had seen. He never tired of recounting the delighted shriek of horror from the audience when King Kong appeared on the Empire State Building. Donald was also allowed to buy what Father condemned as Penny Dreadfuls. So, again, I should have to listen to the current episode, bought in Rhyl — the one about the boy trapped in the web of a giant spider.

Fortunately for me, the poisons room contained my own private world of terror, which put me on level terms with Donald. Pinned to the back of the door, with four drawing pins, was Father's Poisons List 1925, First and Second Schedules. No monster on Donald's cinema screen, whether created by Baron Frankenstein or by anybody else, could have given me more pleasure than the thrill I got from studying that Poisons List. ARSENIC, it read at the top, as a kind of opening jolt, with the accompanying phrase HALIDES OF ARSENIC — better than just ARSENIC, it seemed to me. A little further down the list came CYANIDES, followed by the splendid DOUBLE CYANIDES OF MERCURY. And, for my money, no word sounded more chilling than the tailender, STRYCHNINE, especially with its added refinement, SALTS OF STRYCHNINE. I read and re-read those wonderful schedules, dwelling lovingly on NITRIC ACID and the fatal COMPRESSED HYDROCANIC ACID.

Underneath the locked poison cupboard were two drawers containing magnificent labels bearing huge warnings in blood-red capitals — POISON. GIVES FORTH POISONOUS VAPOURS. KEEP AWAY FROM ALL EXPOSED PARTS. But my absolute favourite of these was the one that read WARNING. CONTAINS ARSENOUS OXIDE. DO NOT GET ON HANDS. WASH HANDS IMMEDIATELY IF IN CONTACT WITH. All in all, I decided, a few minutes with The Poisons List

1925 was more fun than weeks of Dracula-viewing with Donald Rathwell.

'What on earth are you doing up there?'

Father's sudden roar, from the foot of the stairs, interrupted my reverie.

'I'm on my way,' I called, hurrying to the stock room.

'Well, bring a packet of bicarbonate of soda while you're about it,' Father instructed.

The stock room had nothing to commend it. Every shelf exuded plain, boring discomfort. There was simply row upon row of cod-liver oil, cascara, liver pills, assorted laxatives, bicarbonate of soda and, of course, chilblain ointment.

I hurried back to the front shop with the necessary items.

'Alderman Williams is here for his prints,' Father said. Father was standing in his usual position, behind the cabinet at the top end. This was made of mahogany, with gold letters in Latin upon each of the small drawers. Father always pulled out the bottom drawer and rested his left foot upon it.

'Pity you didn't think of calling in the dark room on your way down.'

I began a fresh ascent to the dark room, where films were developed.

'Alderman Williams' photographs, Mr Jenkins,' I called into the blackness of the dark room.

Even on a bank holiday, Mr Jenkins was there, wearing a broken eye-shield as a badge of his profession.

'They're in the Kodak folder, right under your nose, Sunny Jim,' replied Mr Jenkins.

Mr Jenkins had a deathly white appearance. I suppose this was because Father rarely let him out into the light.

Downstairs once more, I handed the photographs to Alderman Williams. Through the open shop door I could see the grim, spectacled face of Mrs Williams, his wife, who taught me scripture at St Mark's Sunday School. She was in the passenger seat of their Baby Austin, holding on to her offensive wire-haired terrier.

'I'm not sure that I've quite mastered that Box Brownie you sold me, Mr Knox Mawer,' said Alderman Williams. 'Or perhaps it was more cloudy than usual at Llandudno this year.'

I felt sorry for Alderman Williams as he returned to his lady wife. Only one photograph had come out at all. And with that you couldn't tell if the grey blodge in the background was Mrs Williams or the Great Orme.

Just then a cloud burst over 9 High Street.

'Quickly — take up the awnings,' Father directed.

From the entry I took out the long heavy pole with a hook on the end.

'Don't forget to put it back immediately,' Father added, 'first nail on the right.' It was quite a business getting the ancient green canvas to fold into the iron brackets on the wall. Back in the shop again, I helped myself to a treacle cough lozenge while Father's attention was elsewhere. He had spotted a young lady smoking, by the cosmetics counter.

'No smoking allowed in these premises, Madam,' she was told.

I hastily immersed myself in a flurry of activity, beginning with the swan-necked display carboys which had to be topped up with coloured water.

'That girl with the cigarette,' Father exploded, 'I do believe she deliberately dropped this sweet paper on the floor.'

With some difficulty he managed to bend down and pick it up himself, since I was busy cleaning the front windows.

These had to be polished every day, like the brass on the sills.

'The front door handle could do with another shine,' Father noted.

Because of the absence of staff on a bank holiday, Father did not go home for lunch. He manned the pharmacy alone while I was despatched to Resthaven to collect his hot meal.

I was required to convey the hot meal from Resthaven to the shop in a large brown leather suitcase.

'Carried horizontally,' Father emphasised. Edith had to have the menu ready in the kitchen for my collection at precisely 12.55 pm.

'And make sure it's piping hot,' had been another of Father's strictures.

Two dangerously heated plates were needed to sustain the required temperature. The bottom one contained meat, potatoes, two vegetables and gravy. Alongside went a starched napkin, in Father's silver ring. Partitioned off behind rolled-up copies of the *Wrexham Leader* were two dishes of loganberries and custard. There was also a side plate, for me; and a considerable quantity of cutlery.

'At least you've not spilt the gravy this time,' Father said as he meticulously portioned out my share.

We had to eat the meal standing up, using a space specially cleared on the proprietary counter, between the Beecham's Pills and the barley water.

'You'd best get cleaning up the back,' Father directed after lunch.

'There'll not be much custom in the front shop.'

'Up the back' comprised two crypt-like rooms with stone floors. These were encrusted with the sediment of ages, hard as iron. The first room had once been a kitchen where the eighteenth-century apothecary had used a pestle and mortar in front of the huge open fireplace. The fireplace was still in use for the burning of old packing cases. There was a long plain wooden table which it was my first job to scrub. The other room, with no windows, was full of tea chests from which bits of straw blew back in my face from the draught up the entry.

It was never possible to make any impression upon the blackened stone flags. I was chipping away — at my doomed and hopeless task — when I heard the metallic clack of Father's heels outside.

'Time to lock up,' he announced.

My spirits would have risen at this news had I not been aware of Father's plan for 'after high tea'.

'You'll be helping with my election campaign,' he had reminded me.

The election campaign, to which the bank holiday evening was devoted, was not for Parliament. In Father's view it was far more important than that. His seat on the Pharmaceutical Council of Great Britain was at stake.

A printed address from him had to go out to all the pharmacists in the country. This promised the electorate an appallingly grim future if he were not re-elected.

'You would think, Clara,' Father burst forth, 'that, by now, this boy could stick on a postage stamp.'

I can't think how I managed it. Yet every time I seemed to get one of the stamps upside down. Getting King George the Fifth — the King Emperor — upside down, was, according to Father, a form of treason. A familiar chorus tinkled across from the wireless set.

> It's Monday night at eight o'clock.
> Oh, can't you hear the chimes?
> Inviting you to take an easy chair.

There was to be no easy chair for me. I was packed off upstairs to bed.

I made sure my door was not altogether closed so that a ray of landing light came in, while from the dining-room I could hear the strains of the radio programme drifting faintly upstairs, always a consolation. The BBC ladies were signing off now.

So goodnight everybody
It's time to say goodnight.
Monday night at eight is closing down.

I closed my eyes upon another bank holiday with
Father, and slipped immediately into a dream of being at
the fair with Donald and Muriel Rathwell. We were taking
pot shots at a row of carboys, and Mr Jenkins, from the
dark room, was dispensing ice-cream.

CHAPTER 8

THE WONDERS OF WALES

Pistyll Rhaedr, Wrexham Steeple,
Snowdon Mountain, without its people
Overton yew trees, St Winifred's Well,
Llangollen bridge and Gresford Bell.

Miss Punchard's class, with me in the second row along-side Donald Rathwell, sat droning out these curious lines (author anonymous) which were taught to every school-child in North Wales. We then had to point out their whereabouts on the classroom map of the Principality. Those of us fortunate enough to have seen any of the 'Wonders' were invited to describe their impressions to the rest of the form. It was an item in our school itinerary that met with little enthusiasm from Father.

'Seven Wonders of Wales!' he snorted. 'They'd be better known as the Seven Disappointments.'

Despite Father's protests, it seemed that the Seven Wonders were to form the itinerary of the family 'mystery tour' arranged by the Masonic Lodge for Whit Saturday. Transport was provided by Mr Sugg, a local charabanc owner, known as Why Walk Sugg, because of his slogan, WHY WALK WHEN YOU CAN RIDE WITH ME?

It was a fine sunny morning when we set out from Wrexham, a party of thirty or so, parents and children. We rattled through Oswestry, then the angular bus plunged into the wooded countryside, pulling up at the end of a sharp valley.

'Pistyll Rhaedr,' pronounced Mr Sugg, in an explosion of Welsh consonants.

'Most famous falls in Wales.'

Getting out, we found ourselves looking across the little wooden bridge at the foaming cataract pouring between trees and rocks from the mountain heights above.

'Magnificent,' extolled Worshipful Brother Rathwell.

'God's handiwork indeed,' added Mrs Rathwell.

There was a murmur of appreciation all round, broken by a querulous voice from the rear.

'Surely,' Father remarked, 'Wales is able to do better than this.'

He rounded on Mrs Rathwell.

'You only have to think of Niagara Falls. No less than two thousand six hundred feet across. Did you know that?'

Father always had a boggling store of facts and figures in the back of his mind, gleaned from Cassell's *Complete Educator*, which he liked to discharge at strategic moments. There was a crestfallen silence. Mr Sugg moved us rapidly on to the next port of call, at Bedgellert, where the rain was falling steadily over the peaks of Snowdonia.

From under his umbrella, Father pointed in the direction of Snowdon itself.

'Have you ever seen anything like that, Clara?'

'Very nice, George,' Mother said, peering through the mist. 'Not that I can see it very well.'

'That's just the point, woman!' he thundered. 'Nobody can. Complete let-down.'

It was the cue for a picnic lunch — tomato sandwiches and cream buns with raspberry pop. Father sat on a rock eating a duck egg, 'hardboiled fifteen minutes'.

We returned along the Holyhead road to Llangollen Bridge. The traffic was thick with Baby Austins and Hundred Pound Fords. People crowded the ice-cream stalls by the River Dee. The bridge itself was restricted to one-way traffic.

'A hopeless bottle-neck,' Father declared. 'How anyone could design this as a major crossing point over the Dee valley defeats me.'

The bus had come to a halt. To my amazement, Father was at the door poised to descend.

'Look careful, Mr Knox Mawer,' called Mr Sugg, 'we don't want you getting run over, do we?' The silence on the bus indicated a measure of disagreement on this point. One or two passengers looked hopefully towards the on-coming traffic. Father was determined to prove for himself the inadequacy of Bishop Trevor's medieval masterpiece. Holding up his hand, he performed a measured tread to the parapet on the other side and back again.

'It's barely five paces across,' he reported, boarding the bus again.

'That's not something you read in the guide-books.'

From my point of view, the outing had been a nerve-racking ordeal. Whatever would Father do next? Donald Rathwell's sniggers were increasingly hard to bear. Perhaps our fourth stop, Overton churchyard, would be less provocative. It struck me as a gloomy place, darkly over-shadowed by huge yew trees of an immense age. According to Mr Sugg, the branches had once made excellent bows for the archers recruited by Henry V in preparation for Agincourt.

'And still in marvellous condition,' agreed Mrs Rathwell.

'Badly neglected if you ask me,' said Father, snapping his close-view spectacles back into their case.

Brother Thomas, the Wrexham outfitter, brought out a tape measure and tried to encircle the trunk of the largest tree.

'They do say the circumference is over twenty feet,' he

declared. A particularly spiky branch caught him unawares and he sprang back with an unmasonic oath.

'I could have told you that would happen,' said Father, examining the deep scratch on Mr Thomas's wrist. He applied a strip of plaster from his breast pocket to the injury. 'Cattle sometimes die after being in contact with yew-leaves,' he warned. 'If you feel paralysis coming on, we can always drop you off at the War Memorial Hospital.'

Gresford church was not far away. Here we were greeted by the sound of the famous peal. 'The chimes are noted for their sweetness,' the Master Bellringer lectured his attentive audience. Father had come prepared. He opened a small packet from his waistcoat pocket and brought out a pair of Dr Collis Brown's Improved Earplugs.

'Guaranteed to keep out disturbing sound,' he explained.

The Master Bellringer was preparing to take the party up the bell tower. There was no question of Father accompanying them, and I was told that I might not go either. 'You can go completely mad in a bell tower,' Father said. I was very impressed. Perhaps Mr Rathwell would emerge looking like the picture I had seen outside the Hippodrome Cinema of the Hunchback of Notre Dame. The coach party remained up in the bell tower for a surprising length of time, in view of the risks I thought they were taking.

'At least they won't have time now to bother with St Winifred's Well,' Father said to Mother as we waited in the charabanc. He was mistaken. All too soon, we were chugging along the road to Holywell. I ventured to ask Father what was this well.

'It's nothing but a hotbed of Romish superstition,' he replied. 'Certainly not worth getting out for,' he told the company at large. He was outvoted. The next moment we were all crowded into the sixteenth-century chapel that overlooked the famous pool. Upon the vaulted walls, various pilgrims had scratched the details of their visit.

'November 12th 1789 read one inscription miraculously cured of ye goute. Thanks be to Sainte Winifred.' Someone rashly tried a joke at Father's expense.

'Good job she didn't set up a chemist shop in the High Street, Brother Knox.'

Father was not amused. Under the cloud of his disapproval we returned to our starting point in Wrexham.

Here Father spent some time pointing out how badly the stone of Wrexham Steeple had weathered over the centuries. But this was not his only carp.

'It's no good,' he said to Mrs Rathwell, 'no good at all!'

'How do you mean?' she asked.

Father pointed to the gilded clock-face in the steeple. It had not occurred to the medieval craftsman that this masterpiece would one day be masked by the roof of the Midland Bank and so not visible to Father in the shop.

The following year, Father came forward with a new suggestion. 'As a venue,' he said 'nothing, simply nothing could be more worthwhile than a tour of the chemical works at Cefn.'

The sinister chimneys of the works had been letting out noxious fumes for a hundred years, and employees forced to live in the vicinity were an object of local sympathy.

'They make enough sulphuric acid there to supply not only home but foreign markets as well,' Father urged. 'And in the very latest of laboratories.'

'Perhaps another time, Brother,' soothed Mr Rathwell.

'Never put off to the morrow what can be arranged today,' came the reply.

It was to no avail. His suggestion was turned down.

'Then I shall go myself,' he declared. 'And that boy can come along with me,' he added, as an afterthought.

For once Mother spoke out.

'Not with his chest, dear,' she said.

On his return, Father dubbed the works the Eighth Wonder of Wales. 'Worth all the rest of them put together.'

The Welsh Tourist Board has yet to agree with Father's view. But then his was usually a minority opinion; ahead of his time, maybe.

CHAPTER 9

FATHER AT PLAY

Upon the shaky top shelf of Father's revolving bookcase stood four green clothbound volumes — *The Encyclopaedia of Sport and Games*, edited by the Earl of Suffolk and Berkshire. The ponderous appearance of these tomes epitomised Father's approach to his meticulously rationed spells of recreation.

In volume four, 'Rackets to Zebra', there was a section entitled 'Ratting' by Brigadier J. Watson, pictured wearing the obligatory bowler hat. The Brigadier opened his treatise with the surprising observation, 'Every sportsman has indulged in ratting at some time or another,' and concluded with the information — 'to find a dead rat, go to the butchers and catch a dozen bluebottles. Slip them into a glass jar, tying a bit of rag over the mouth. Proceed to the room where the smell is, shut the door behind you, and let loose your pack of flies. They will go buzzing round and round, and after a time will all settle on the self-same spot. Under that particular spot, to an inch, is the dead rat.'

I am unsure how far Father put this advice into practice, and do not recall a visit to our family butcher — fellow Mason, D. J. Morgan — for the entrapment of bluebottles. Yet Father certainly annotated the Brigadier's article with marginal notes, using his silver propelling pencil. Eventually he plunged into the field of sporting journalism himself. In the 1931 Christmas number of *The Chemist and Druggist*, he published a paper entitled 'Getting to Grips with the Rising Rat Problem', in which he outlined his

own experiments with arsenic and strychnine. One stat-
istic he failed to mention, in his article, was the sudden
incidence of early mortality among domestic pets in the
Grosvenor Road area.

Fortunately he did not confine his sporting life to ratting. Hockey became a crusading interest, stemming from
a belief that the game had become the 'unwarranted pre-
serve' of 'girls in gymslips'. He sponsored his own men's
team, ordering a special uniform from the Army Surplus
Store. This comprised a belligerent combination of black
shirts, khaki shorts, red stockings and brown (ex-officers')
boots. Naturally, he elected himself club president for life,
carefully running no risk of deposition, since he held the
key to the private repository where the equipment was
stored. Somewhat to Mother's dismay, the eleven hockey
sticks, spare balls, and goalkeepers pads were securely
wedged into the oak settle in the hall.

But that was not quite all that Father kept in the chest,
by way of sporting gear. There was also his tennis racquet.
With tennis, too, Father consulted the magnum opus of
the Earl of Suffolk and Berkshire. In volume three of the
Encyclopaedia of Sport and Games, on page 115, the late
Mr Foy was shown demonstrating what he termed the
American or colonial grip for the forehand return off the
bounce. Father often quoted Mr Foy on the impropriety
of the volley. 'It is rank bad form,' he used to read, from
page 116, 'to hit the ball before it strikes the ground.'

'My own opinion exactly,' Father said, taking up his
own racquet which was of identically the same design as
Mr Foy's.

Pear-shaped, and with quaintly carved wings at the end
of the handle, the instrument was unbelievably heavy.
This racquet he used on the public courts in Belle Vue
Park, Bradley Road. His appearance invariably attracted
a crowd of spectators. This may have been partly due to
his dress. Instead of his usual wing collar and dark grey

suit, Father wore a pair of yellowing cricket flannels, which Mother had let out to accommodate what was known as the waist-line. Over and above, he wore a white linen shirt, which billowed out like a vast marquee.

When it came to footwear, there was a regular confrontation.

'What on earth is wrong?' Father demanded, every time the attendant complained.

'It's just that you're supposed to wear tennis shoes, Mr Knox Mawer,' insisted the official.

'Are you employed by the Corporation?'

'Yes, I am.'

'Then kindly refer your objection to the Mayor.'

The problem was that Father insisted upon wearing his cricket boots. These were made of calf and, as Father never failed to point out, 'extremely expensive'.

The attendant, who was accustomed to Father's tantrums, remained calm. I can remember the names of some of the mayors of Wrexham to whom Father angrily referred — Councillor Powell, the solicitor, Councillor Price, the grocer, Councillor Probert, the leather merchant.

'Close friends of mine, I'll have you know.'

This was palpably untrue. I'm afraid Father had no friends who could so be termed, either close or distant.

'This court is made of asphalt, is it not?'

'As you can see.'

'Well how then,' Father thundered, 'can the Mayor, let alone the Corporation, maintain that an expensive pair of cricket boots could possibly do it any harm?'

By this time the attendant had grown tired of the polemics and wandered over to watch the players on the nearby bowling green.

During this exchange I remained on the pavilion steps pretending to retie my plimsolls. Our opponents, meanwhile, Donald Rathwell and his father, were already on the court. They clearly enjoyed the commotion. It was to their advantage that Father worked himself up in these preliminaries so that he had lost all concentration for the game.

'Perhaps you'd better serve, Worshipful Brother Knox Mawer,' suggested Mr Rathwell.

Clearing his throat and standing well back against the wire, Father threw the ball to an enormous height, then brought the racquet down with a flat crashing movement. With this kind of force behind, both services flew well beyond the service area, and we usually lost the match. I never minded, so long as the uppish Donald Rathwell had been hit by one of Father's serves, preferably upon the nose.

The dramatic tension of partnering Father at tennis was only equalled by the embarrassment of being taken along by him to the Wrexham Football Ground. For a short period, Father was a director of the club, a brief venture, because the finances of Wrexham Football Club rested upon foundations as flimsy as the Pharmacy at 9 High Street.

Director or not, Father occupied a central seat in the stand, alongside Worshipful Brother George Turney, the wholesaler, from whom Father purchased so much barbed wire 'in bulk'. It was Mr Turney's lethal product, massed on the walls of Resthaven, that gave Father's garden the appearance of a concentration camp. Mr Turney was as sharp in manner as his barbed wire, and, together, the two portly Worshipful Brethren in the stand kept up a constant stream of criticism of the local team, struggling to retain its place at the bottom of the Third Division.

But there was a far worse source of discomfiture from my point of view. Father never took his seat at the Ground without a wooden box of apples under his arm, which it was my job to distribute to neighbouring spectators, young and old, on the adjoining benches. The trouble was that Father's apples were badly tainted with creosote. This was because he stored them in the shed alongside the drum of creosote, purchased, now I come to think about it, from Worshipful Brother George Turney. Today's spectators would ridicule the very idea of free apples, let alone polluted ones. At that time politeness prevailed. The apples were accepted, but after an initial bite, hastily discarded under the benches. By the end of the match, Father's section of the stand closely resembled Covent Garden at the close of a busy day's trading.

Why, I ask myself, did Father not behave like other parents? How was it that he had to be different from the normal fathers of my friends? Those wretched apples were just another blush-making example of his shattering inability to conform.

It was after accompanying Father home from a football match that he made a memorable pronouncement. We were having supper and he was serving out what he called the cold collation.

'This boy, Clara,' he said looking up suddenly, 'walks like a duck.' Next morning I discovered the 1931 Keep Fit Movement Chart pinned to my bedroom door. Father had ringed the upper left corner with his silver propelling pencil. EXERCISES FOR STRAIGHTENING THE SPINE, it read.

Another exercise for straightening my spine was swimming. Of all Father's recreational activities, this was the one I most disliked.

'Are we ready for a dip, then?' came the dread announcement from the hall. 'All work and no play makes Jack a dull boy,' Aunty Carrie never failed to point out. I would have been happy to remain a dull boy rather than visit the Wrexham Public Baths.

They stood in the dingiest street of the town, Tuttle Street, a hideous construction of carrot-coloured Ruabon brick. The pool reeked of chlorine. There were huge iron girders above, echoing to the screams and yells of those children underneath who could swim. I, of course, could not.

In a separate cubicle alongside Father's I changed into a hopelessly large green costume with shoulder straps. This had once belonged to Aunty Carrie. As for Father in his bathing suit of black and yellow stripes, he looked like an enormous wasp. What made him look especially petrifying was the rubber bathing cap on his head. It reminded me of the headgear worn by the axeman in the print of The Execution of Lady Jane Gray on our landing wall.

Execution struck me as infinitely preferable to that stinging water in my eyes and the ominous signal from Father to those about me, 'Let him go.'

I sank like a stone. While Father swam fifteen lengths with a strong crawl I was dismissed to the side bench. There I sat, ignominiously surrounded by large giggling wet girls, who could both swim and dive, until it was time to go.

Back home at the supper table Father took up the carving knife. 'One thing puzzles me, Clara,' he said, darting his eyes briefly in my direction, 'the boy walks like a duck, we all agree. Why at least can't he swim like one!'

He gave a short sharp bark — Father's equivalent to a laugh — and poured me a dash of ginger beer.

CHAPTER 10

LODGE

It was Donald Rathwell's idea.

'Gosh,' I said, when he told me The Plan. 'We'd better not get caught.'

He should have known the risks, because Aunty Carrie had warned him too.

'Ronnie's right, Donald,' she had said. 'Them Freemasons is a dangerous lot. The first thing they do is blacken your dickie. Everyone knows that!'

But Donald had a special interest in penetrating the secrets of the Craft. Mr Rathwell was a leading Mason and almost as fanatical about the Square and Compass Lodge as Father. Donald and I used to watch them leaving together, in Mr Rathwell's car, on Lodge Night. Each carried a sealed leather case of midget size, though large enough, we could see, for the necessary paintbrush and the black boot-polish.

'I know where they all meet to do it,' Donald boasted.

After school, he took me to the corner of Prince Arthur Street, Wrexham, and pointed out the old chapel.

'In there,' he said.

'Gosh,' I said again. 'Not a church!'

'They don't seem to do it until after dark,' Donald said, 'and it's a good place to hide. I got in last Saturday morning, easy. When the cleaning ladies were there. Climbed right up into the organ loft and out again without being seen.'

On the following Friday, Mrs Rathwell invited me to

supper with Donald. That was when he put the pressure on. 'Your Dad will never know.'

Dad! In this particular context the word shocked me. None of us at home ever referred to the head of the household in that way. To me it seemed extraordinary when I heard friends dismissively refer to Good Old Pop, the Old Man, or worst of all, Pa. So far as I was concerned it always had been and always would be Father.

'Don't be such a weed,' Donald continued. 'We'll never get such a good chance again,' he insisted. 'Your mother isn't expecting you back until late. I'm allowed to go to the cinema. And I'm allowed to go to Lindseys for fish and chips afterwards. That's what I'll tell my folks we're doing.'

Mrs Rathwell popped her head around the door of Donald's bedroom.

'It's a Will Hay film, Mum, called *Boys will be Boys*,' Donald told her, 'it's supposed to be very funny.'

Mrs Rathwell looked at me doubtfully.

'I'm not sure that your father would . . .'

'You'll not tell him *anything*,' Donald interrupted, 'will you Mum?'

'Well, as both your fathers will be out amusing themselves, I don't see why you shouldn't do the same.'

She smiled at me.

'I expect Mrs Knox Mawer feels the way I do, Ronnie,' she said. 'We're both what I call masonic widows. Those two men of ours spend half their time at that Square and Compass Lodge.'

Mrs Rathwell dashed off to answer the telephone — the Rathwells were the only family I knew to have a telephone — just as Donald exploded into helpless laughter.

'An' we'll be there too.'

Mrs Rathwell supplied Donald with half a crown and I hurried out after him, pulling on my school cap.

'Where are you two off to in such a hurry?' demanded a loud voice. We'd collided at the Rathwells' front gate with a bicycle belonging to the lamplighter, who had been reaching up from the saddle to pull down the gas mantle on the lampost. Donald's father peered down from the window of his bedroom where he was tying on his black Masonic tie.

'They're going to the Odeon cinema,' his wife called up the stairs.

Mr Rathwell opened the window.

'If they don't look where they're going,' he warned, 'they'll end up at the War Memorial hospital.' He was always a one for jokes.

It was lucky for us that it was already dark, because we were able to shin up the back wall into the chapel grounds unseen.

'Was-at?' Donald hissed over his shoulder.

'Sorry,' I gasped. As usual when under strain, my aniseed ball had gone down the wrong way.

The church clock chimed six as we darted through the shadows. The Square and Compass Lodge met at six-thirty.

'No sign of the caretaker anyway,' Donald reported. He tried the front door. It was unlocked.

'Look sharp now,' he said.

With considerable trepidation I followed on his heels and reached the organ loft more or less in one piece.

'Have a pear-drop,' Donald said.

Rigid with fear, I could barely manage a shake of the head. I was still coping with the after-effects of the aniseed ball.

'There's somebody come in,' Donald whispered. I peered down through a gap in the floorboards.

'It's old Mr Camp,' I said, recognising the white-haired organist from the parish church in his Masonic regalia — a short white 'cooking apron' as Donald called it.

'If he starts to play through these organ pipes,' I told Donald, 'we'll be suffocated.'

'There isn't an organ anymore,' Donald replied crushingly, 'only a harmonium.'

Mr Camp had switched on the lights beneath us. He sat at the harmonium and began to practise. Meanwhile the hall began to fill with other men similarly dressed in dinner jackets and masonic aprons.

'That's Mr Thornton,' Donald said, identifying the proprietor of Thornton's Electrical Stores. Mr Thornton was smoothing out a large carpet of black and white squares. Another familiar figure was Mr Edwards, the bank manager. He normally wore a hat like Mr Anthony Eden whom he vaguely resembled, except that his bulbous nose made him far less handsome.

Assisted by Mr Davies, the optician, the bank manager was setting up a wooden pillar and lighting candles by it. According to Donald this was what they called 'the masonic temple'.

A number of impressively carved chairs were positioned around the tesselated border of the carpet. From the beam in the centre, above, was hung a large letter G.

'My father's name is George,' I told Donald excitedly.

'G is for God, idiot,' he replied with a snort.

A candlestick was placed alongside one of the chairs and a second candlestick alongside another. In front of the biggest chair of all was a kneeling stool.

'Shine the torch,' Donald instructed. His prize trophy was the pack of printed cards he had stolen from the drawer of his father's desk.

'Dad calls them his cribs,' Donald explained. 'Lucky he doesn't need them any more so he won't even notice they've gone.'

Just then my heart stopped beating. A large figure, wearing, in addition to his apron, an elaborately ornamented halter which made him look like a cart horse, was advancing up the aisle.

'It's Father!' I breathed.

Father was also wearing gauntlets. He seated himself in the largest and most ornate chair of all. 'He's called the Worshipful Master,' Donald said. 'Everyone has to worship him.'

I could imagine this quite easily. God and Father had always been interchangeable figures in my experience.

'My dad's next in line,' Donald added, in case I was getting too cocky.

Mr Rathwell, similarly attired, had followed Father into the Temple and was now positioned in a slightly smaller chair at the opposite side of the Lodge. The door was closed and a stout gentleman took up his position by it.

'Isn't that Mr Wallace the dentist?' I enquired.

It was Mr Wallace. He was armed with a large dagger, even more formidable than the drill he usually flourished when I sat helpless in his chair.

Donald consulted one of the cribs.

'They're going to irritate someone into the Lodge,' he said, 'that's what they're going to do.' He looked more closely. 'Sorry — in-it-iate. That means they're going to make him into a Mason.'

'And do what Aunty Carrie said?' I asked.

'That's right,' said Donald.

'But why does he need a dagger?' I persisted.

Donald smiled knowingly.

'Maybe if they get any trouble, they'll cut it right off,' he said.

The scene below resembled a photograph I had seen in *The Illustrated London News*. THE HOLY FATHER IN SOLEMN ENCLAVE, the caption had read. The Pope was seated upon an enormous throne with various church dignitaries assembled in their respective positions about him. Father as Pope was a new concept to me, but again a totally believable one. Even at that moment he raised what looked like a large ecclesiastical mallet and dropped it heavily on the altar-like desk in front of him. This knock was repeated by Mr Rathwell with his knuckles on a table.

'Brethren,' said Father, 'assist me to open the Lodge.'

Everybody rose.

'Brother Thornton,' Father continued, 'what is the first care of every Mason?'

'To see that the Lodge is properly tyled,' came the answer.

'What's tyled?' hissed Donald.

'Something to do with bathrooms,' I replied helpfully.

'Direct that duty to be done,' Father decreed.

Mr Wallace went to the door and, without opening it, gave three knocks.

These were answered from the other side.

'Brother Rathwell,' said Mr Wallace, 'the Lodge is properly tyled.'

Donald and I were following the lines on the crib cards, rather like David Thomas, the form swot, who did the prompting for the school play every year.

'Brother Rathwell,' Father called out, 'what is the next care?'

'To see that none but Masons are present,' Mr Rathwell replied.

These words struck a chill of fear in both of us.

Three knocks sounded from outside the chapel door. These were returned from inside by Mr Wallace.

'Enquire who wants admission,' Father directed.

'Whom have you there?' Mr Wallace called through the closed door. A muffled voice answered from the other side. 'A poor candidate in a state of darkness humbly soliciting to be admitted to the mysteries and privileges of Freemasonry.'

'Halt,' said Mr Wallace, 'while I report to the Worshipful Master.'

He took a step backwards and made an ominous throat-slitting sign, like the one demonstrated by the escaped convict to Pip in *Great Expectations*, our set book that term.

Father spoke again.

'Let the candidate be admitted in due form.'

Mr Wallace opened the door. Donald clutched my arm.

'Golly,' he exclaimed, 'it's Piggy Nichols, the Form-Master!'

At first I thought he was joking. Then slowly the truth dawned. Despite the fact that he was blindfolded, there was no mistaking that snarling countenance under the clipped russet dome. When I'd last seen him, he was wearing his usual mortar board and black gown. There he was now in an extraordinary state of undress. His collarless shirt was unbuttoned, displaying a revoltingly hairy chest. His right sleeve was rolled up above the elbow, while his left trouser leg was wrapped ingloriously above the knee. On his right foot he was wearing a tattered slipper instead of his neatly polished shoe.

'Look at his neck,' Donald said. 'He's got a noose around it.'

I don't think either of us wanted Piggy Nichols to be actually hanged, but a bit of torture was a different thing. We both of us held our breath as Mr Wallace pricked Piggy's throat with the point of the dagger.

'Do you feel anything?'he asked him.

'Yes,' Piggy replied.

'Good,' said Donald with some feeling. His last mark for algebra had been an E, punished by Piggy with five hundred lines.

'Brother Rathwell,' Father proceeded, 'instruct the candidate to advance to the pedestal in due form.'

Their hapless victim was made to perform a series of steps as though in a kind of hopscotch game.

'Kneel on your left knee, your right foot formed in a square,' Father ordered in his deepest growl. This, we were delighted to see, caused him obvious discomfort. Then something called the tools of the trade were handed to him.

'I present to your naked left breast,' Father said, 'a pair of compasses.'

'Is that because he can teach geometry?' I asked Donald.

'No,' said Donald, consulting a crib card. 'It's all down here. Part of the ceremony.'

The next minute Father had Piggy Nichols repeating an unforgettable oath.

'I, John Nichols, do swear that I will never reveal the secrets of Masonry under no less a penalty than of having my throat cut across, my tongue torn out by the root, and buried in the sand of the sea at low water mark, or a cable's length from the shore, where the tide regularly ebbs and flows in twenty-four hours.'

Donald and I looked at each other speechless. Piggy Nichols with his tongue torn out was something even we have never imagined in our wildest dreams.

The blindfold was next removed from the candidate's eyes and Father presented him with his Masonic apron.

'You are now at liberty,' he told him, 'to retire in order to restore yourself to your personal comfort.'

'That means he can go to the lav,' Donald sniggered.

With Mr Nichols outside, a number of sinister preparations were made for his return. Mr Thornton laid a sheet upon the floor near to Father's pedestal. Donald pushed against me to look more closely and nearly fell out of the loft. On the sheet was drawn a large skull and crossbones!

'Poor old Piggy,' Donald said. 'But you can't say he didn't deserve it.'

Our Form-Master was readmitted to the Temple and there followed an even more sensational spectacle. It was really his turn for punishment now.

First of all Mr Wallace aimed a blow at his right temple

with a ruler. Then Mr Rathwell struck him with a spirit level. Finally Father cracked him on the forehead with the fancy mallet. We could see that none of these blows was sufficiently hard to hurt him — they were too light for Donald's taste — but it was a treat to see his prostrate figure lowered into what was obviously meant to be his grave. Mr Camp played the 'Dead March' on the harmonium while his brother Masons wrapped the body in the skull and crossbones sheet. There was a suspenseful moment when Brothers Thornton and Rathwell seemed to be trying to restore the candidate to life. The attempt failed. It was Father's turn. Solemnly he approached Mr Nichols' prone body. With a series of incantations he applied a kind of fireman's lift.

'What is he doing?' I said to Donald.

'Resurrecting him,' said Donald succinctly.

He was right. The next minute, a considerably subdued Mr Nichols was upright again.

We reckoned the humiliation of our detested beak was complete when he was finally obliged to goose-step, still undressed, all the way around the Lodge.

'Brethren,' said Father, 'assist me now to close the Lodge.'

That was the final curtain, and as the Masons were moving out into the annexe of the chapel, for their Masonic dinner, Donald and I made our escape.

Donald hid the crib cards in his father's toolshed. During the following months, behind the closed doors of the Rathwells' toolshed, we were able to relive the exciting ceremony in every detail. Donald and I played the star roles of Father and Piggy Nichols. I preferred to do the part of Mr Nichols, never feeling quite at home being God.

Our game had a simple name. LODGE.

CHAPTER 11

THE IDES OF MARCH

On Saturday mornings, Donald Rathwell never missed Gene Autrey, the Singing Cowboy, at the Odeon Cinema in Brook Street. For me there was no question of escaping the confines of home. Propped up against the cutlery case on the sideboard stood Father's dismal list of Saturday jobs.

1 Weed shrubbery.
2 Clean out pigeon droppings.
3 Pick up bits in conservatory.
4 Sweep back yard.
5 Brush cellar steps.

Pinned to the back of the list was a cutting from UNCLE GEOFF'S CORNER in the *Wrexham Leader*.

CHILDREN! WHAT DO YOU KNOW ABOUT YOUR WELSH PATRON SAINT? ENTRIES BY ST DAVID'S DAY MARCH 1ST.

Underneath, Father had written with his silver propelling pencil, 'What do *you* know? I shall need to see your entry as soon as possible.'

After lunch, when Father was ensconced in his Director's box at the Wrexham Football Ground, skipping the last of the cellar steps, I hurried down to the public library, a musty emporium in the Beast Market.

'You'll find the *Dictionary of Saints* upstairs in the reference room,' Miss Foulkes, the Assistant Librarian, told me sternly. She wore horn-rimmed spectacles which made her eyes smaller and sinister, like black marbles. Unfortunately, St David was afforded only three lines in the dictionary: 'Born 6th century. Founded Welsh monasteries. The book upon which other details of his life have been founded is now discredited.'

I did my best with this meagre entry, adding, by a stretch of imagination, 'Played a harp, had a long white beard, and rode a horse like the singing cowboy.'

'Pathetic,' was Father's verdict on my work. 'I'd be ashamed to let Worshipful Brother Lerry see this!'

How was I to know that Uncle Geoff was Mr G. G. Lerry, editor of the *Wrexham Leader*, and a fellow Mason?

Father, unlike Uncle Geoff — a homegrown Wrexhamian — had been born on the shores of the North Sea. Long resident in the Principality, however, he now considered himself a true Welshman. As with everything else, he went to extremes about it.

'Let me hear that boy recite the Welsh National Anthem,' he said, over breakfast on St David's Day. He had already ensured that the Red Dragon was rampant on the flagpole in the front garden.

Appropriately enough, it was at that time of year, the beginning of March, that Father chose to abandon his sidesman's pew at Wrexham Parish Church, in the cause of Welsh culture. He commandeered a seat in the front row of the Welsh Chapel in Rhosddu Road. So unexpected was his visit that Dai Evans, the organ blower, stopped pumping at the sight of him. There was panic among the all-ladies choir, ruining the first verse in Welsh of *Lead Me O Thou Great Jehovah*.

'This is something of a surprise,' said the minister, Mr Gwilliam Rees, at the door.

Father's reply was not designed to impress Mr Rees with his spiritual conversion to Nonconformity.

'I'm only here to pick up some Welsh, Mr Rees,' he said, clapping his silk hat back on his head.

Luckily for Mr Rees, on the next Sunday there was an

embarrassing occurrence. Father lost his place and his temper in the psalm.

He began again, using his own English prayer book.

One minute into the pastor's sermon saw him stomping out to the parish church in the next street. He arrived in time to take round the plate — for a bumper collection. The vicar beamed. He relied upon Father's glare in thrusting forward the collection plate, whenever a worshipper was minded to substitute a threepenny bit for sixpence. This greatly enhanced the parish church revenue.

While Father never succeeded in mastering Welsh, this did not diminish his enthusiasm for the national day of Wales. By tradition, the correct emblem was of course the leek. But the safety-pin, on the giant specimen chosen for me by Aunty Carrie, tore a hole in the lapel of my green school blazer.

'Your father will find you a daffodil,' she said, putting a hasty stitch into the damage.

'Fair daffodils, we weep to see thee haste away so soon,' Father intoned, rather red in face, and obviously much moved, as he emerged from his overheated greenhouse with a jaded bloom.

Father's daffodils faded even more rapidly than Robert Herrick's. Mr Nichols, the Form-Master, had made me write out the Herrick poem about daffodils for not paying attention.

'Beware the Ides of March,' he rasped, tapping out a topical Shakespearian metre on the back of my neck with a ruler. I had no idea what the Ides were, although I knew what he meant by 'beware of March'. It was a time of year filled with foreboding as far as I was concerned, a series of pitfalls from start to finish.

'Which of your little luxuries have you given up?' the vicar invariably enquired of me. 'For Lent, I mean?'

I thought hard. What luxury was there at Resthaven to be given up? It was always Lent at Resthaven. In any case, a more striking form of penance lay ahead. That was the Cross-Country March Marathon organised by Mr Nichols.

'His only hope of getting in the first three, and not disgracing the family,' Father had said, 'is to keep ahead of the field.'

Obeying his dictum proved to be my first mistake. Instead of settling into a sensible long-distance rhythm, I sprinted across the playing grounds way in front of the rest of the competitors, arriving breathless at the entrance to Acton Park.

TRESPASSERS WILL BE PROSECUTED, read the notice by the crested gates. Obediently, I veered off to circumnavigate the park walls in another pointless burst of speed.

That was my second error.

When I finally collapsed, totally winded, into a pile of nettles, I found that I was entirely alone.

It was raining and a heavy mist had formed. I assumed that the rest of the pack had gone by, since it was no longer possible to see beyond a couple of yards. 'Circle the Gresford Mere,' Mr Nichols had instructed, 'and then back to the pavilion by the same route.'

Gresford Mere lay immediately to the east of Acton Park. By the time I had circled the mere I was almost in need of an ambulance. I took off my gym shoes and bathed my feet in the water, before embarking on the retreat at an invalid's pace.

The fog had lifted by the time I made it to the rugby field. Mr Nichols was standing on the steps of the pavilion with a number of other runners. The race had clearly been over for some time. If I could retrieve my clothes from the changing room without being seen, I thought a degree of humiliation might be avoided.

As I climbed in through the window, I overheard their conversation.

'He definitely started off, sir,' Cook, the house-captain was insisting.

'Oh yes, sir,' added Woolley, the reigning champion, 'I saw him jump when the starting pistol was fired.'

'Well he must have made it by now,' Mr Nichols commented irrascibly, 'even if he came back on all fours!'

Just when I was making my escape, the belt of my raincoat caught in the window latch.

'There he is, sir,' shouted Cook, spotting me trapped in mid-air.

'Where on earth have you been, Mawer?' demanded Mr Nichols.

'Afraid I'm out of condition, sir,' I stammered. 'It's further around the walls of Acton Park than I expected.'

'Around the walls!' Who said anything about going around the walls?'

'But the noticeboard says TRESPASSERS WILL BE PROSECUTED, sir.'

'Do you never listen to anything you're told. Sir Foster Cunliffe gave special permission for the race to go directly across his park!'

He shook his head.

'Anyway, you'd better cut along home straight away. You look like nothing on earth.'

It was dusk by the time I reached the corner of King Street. I crossed the road only to be picked out by the familiar beam of the headlamp on Father's Clino.

'What are you up to, at this late hour?' he wanted to know.

'I'm late back from that mad March Marathon organised by Mr Nichols,' I explained.

He opened the rear door of the car.

'Far too muddy to sit in the front,' was all he said.

Groping my way into the back, I encountered an angry pair of beaks, accompanied by loud quack-quacking.

'There's a couple of ducks in here,' I protested.

'You should feel at home with my Khaki Cambell Runners,' he replied.

The peculiarly named breed constituted the latest acquisition in Father's new burst of enthusiasm as a duck keeper. His shoulders were shaking against the light of the dash-board. Things could have been much worse. Father had made a joke!

In point of fact the bleak winds of March thoroughly suited his temperament.

'March 21st,' he never failed to exclaim, 'officially the first day of spring.'

He directed our gaze through the french window as we sat over high tea.

'Days are getting longer, thank goodness.'

That, to my mind, was the worst part of it. From now on, Father's horticultural concentration camp was no longer in the decent gloom of winter. His plans expanded with the extra hours of daylight, and those plans inevitably included me. There seemed no reason whatsoever for enthusiasm about the spring. And I noticed that Robert Browning — whose poem on the subject I had also had to copy out for Piggy Nichols — seemed to have been careful *not* to be in England 'now that spring is here'. Certainly not in 26 Grosvenor Road, Wrexham.

For Father, on the other hand, the domestic rites of this overpraised season were vigorously welcomed.

'How is the spring cleaning coming along, Clara?' was his persistent cry. Father supervised the dragging out of the well-worn green carpet from the drawing-room. This had to be hung over a clothes-line between the duck shed and and the wash house. I was left to operate the wicker carpet beater.

'Can't he do better than that?' came the shout from the bathroom window.

Down he came to seize the weapon from my hand and

demonstrate a particularly sharp thwack, perfected by years of practice.

He had immense ten-gallon tins of strong disinfectant — with the trade name KILL THAT GERM — delivered from the shop. Under his supervision, these had to be sluiced into all corners of our Victorian hall and passageways.

On one occasion, soon after this operation, Donald Rathwell's sister Muriel turned pale halfway through tea and had to be taken home.

'It's worse than the hospital, Daddy,' we heard her cry, as she was bundled back into the gleaming family car.

Later, on the telephone, Mrs Rathwell explained to Mother that little Muriel had not quite got over her recent tonsilectomy at the War Memorial Surgery. Not that the hospital smell lasted long at Resthaven.

'Giving the house a thoroughly good airing,' was an essential finale to the spring cleaning exercise. Every door and window had to be wedged wide open, while icy wind whistled through each nook and cranny from dawn to bedtime. During this holocaust there was no hope of my finding a quiet corner in which to read.

'Why isn't he outside on a fine day like this?' Father would ask.

He was in his naturalist frame of mind.

'Just look at that red-breast enjoying the sunshine.'

He indicated a small shivering robin which was trying to break the ice upon the stone bird-bath.

Father had designed the bird sanctuary in the form of an obstacle course, 'to give them plenty of exercise.'

A whole series of swings, loops and pulleys had to be negotiated by the most intrepid of his feathered friends, before being awarded a few miserable bacon rinds.

Father watched their struggle with satisfaction.

'In bird life, as in human life, only constant Effort leads to success.'

He turned his attention to the book I had been unsuccessfully trying to conceal behind a cushion.

'*Biggles!*' he exploded. 'By Captain W. E. Johns! Hardly a set book, I imagine, Clara.'

Father examined the fly-leaf of *Biggles*. It had been lent to me by Donald Rathwell. Since it was a birthday present from Worshipful Brother Rathwell to his son, Father was unable to consign it to what he called 'The Dr Barnado Cupboard'. This was where old games, books, and 'all unsuitable presents' were stored prior to removal to the Children's Home, Rhosnessni Lane, at Christmas. *Biggles* was locked away in Grandfather's desk until Donald could collect it.

Father's concern about the state of my school studies was justified. I had carved a modest niche for myself during class breaks as a teller of tales, and spent most of my time during lessons gazing out of the window inventing improbable plots. The annual showdown for my 'deplorable inattention' (Piggy Nichols' words) came with Speech Day. In his capacity as senior school governor, Father played a prominent part in this event. With the other VIP's he attended the buffet lunch in the headmaster's study beforehand. It was there that masters were cross-examined by him as to my results and general lack of progress.

As he stepped up to the lectern, it seemed to me there was a special grimness about his expression. His reading *pince-nez* glinted fearsomely as he swept his gaze over the assembly hall — no doubt with the aim of pinpointing me in the mass of boys.

Luckily I was tucked away in the back row, crouched well down in my chair. From there, Donald Rathwell and I caught only snatches of Father's text — Genesis 22, verses 1–13.

'And God said . . . take now thy son . . . and offer him for a burnt offering,' we heard him say.

'Crikey,' hissed Donald.

Faces craned forward on either side to inspect my reactions.

'And he laid the wood in order and bound his son on the altar,' Father continued.

Donald dug his elbow in my ribs. 'There's plenty of wood in your shed, all right.'

Father's look was like thunder.

Suspense mounted along the row. I could feel myself turning red as I stared down at the service sheet.

'And the angel of the Lord called unto him, lay not thine hand upon the lad,' Father boomed.

'Hear, hear,' muttered Donald with feeling.

'And behold, behind him was a ram, caught in a thicket,' Father's voice rose to a grand finale.

'And he took the ram, and offered him in place of his son.'

'Perhaps one of his ducks'll do instead,' was Donald's comment, as Father closed the heavy black volume with a telling thud.

CHAPTER 12

GOD GAVE US OUR RELATIVES

'God gave us our relatives, thank God for our friends', runs the old adage. It was fortunate, in Father's case, that the Great Architect had at least provided him with a large band of fellow Masons. Friends, as such, did not seem to figure in his life, and his antipathy towards relatives was legendary.

Topping the list of the unloved was Uncle Keith, who had married my Aunt Alice, Father's younger sister. Uncle Keith was blissfully unaware of the extreme indignation his unsolicited visits to Resthaven provoked.

'A-Alice and I didn't like to p-pass the house without calling in, George.'

At the sound of Uncle Keith's stammer, Father would dash up to his bedroom and re-emerge dressed for bee-keeping.

'Well f-fancy that, Alice, every t-time we c-call, George seems to be busy with the hives.'

Father's bee-keeping outfit made him not just inaccessible but macabre. In an effort to keep the veil out of his eyes, he wore on his head a discarded straw boater, obtained from Brother D. J. Morgan, the Wrexham butcher, who had rejected it as no longer of service. Unfortunately the hat was rather bloodstained, and no amount of scrubbing by Edith, our maid, could remove the tell-tale signs of the abattoir. The gruesome headgear was somehow complemented by the blackness of the veil.

Then there were the Baron Frankenstein gloves. In contrast to the veil, these were deathly white in colour, and

made of rubber. Their normal use was in operating thea-
tres and Father sold them at his chemist's shop for that
purpose.

When working with his bee-hives, Father also wore
bicycle clips. To my mind these were strangely connected
with a sensational case I had seen headlined in Father's
Daily Mail, MURDERER WORE BICYCLE CLIPS. Father's less
interesting purpose was merely to prevent the sentinel
bees from crawling up his trouser leg to wreck vengeance
on the one disturbing their peace. However, since
Father — so far as I know — never rode a bicycle in his
life, there was something overtly suspicious about his
bicycle clips.

'C-carry c-carry on, George,' said Uncle Keith, 'we'll
w-watch from behind the French windows.' Uncle was
thinking of Aunt Alice, who had received an especially
nasty sting on her plump arm during their previous visit.

'At least you can lend a hand with the extractor,' Father
countered,

'Rotates the honeycombs, d'you follow — principle of
centrifugal force. Alice can turn the handle. You keep the
cylinder steady.'

Father moved back and to, feeding the extractor with
the wax frames, each containing a number of tiny cells of
honey. Removing the frames from the hives made the
bees extremely angry.

I sympathised with them. For any bee it was exasper-
ating, to say the least, to have one's entire store of honey
removed by a human vandal. Yet Father managed to
cause even greater irritation. His bees were not subjected
to just a single raid, once a year. Every time Aunt Alice
and Uncle Keith called, Father ruthlessly removed from
the hives whatever frugal stock the occupants had managed to build up in the intervening period.

The bees should have known it was a hopeless situation. Uncle Keith had a small private income which he

spent on frequent jaunts in a new Baby Austin motorcar. The jaunts, undertaken in fine weather, always led in the direction of Resthaven, although the ultimate destination was the Royal Hotel, Llangollen.

And at no time did Father's countermeasures deter Uncle Keith and Aunt Alice from calling. So, Father's bees, like the Picts and Scots of Roman times, were constantly harassed into a permanent turmoil of mutinous discontent. Which was why both Aunt Alice and Uncle Keith found themselves a particular target for attack.

'Never mind, Alice,' Mother soothed, as Uncle Keith applied the blue-bag once more to yet another swelling, 'you'll be able to take home a nice jar of honey.' This was never more than a very small jar — grudgingly sanctioned by Father — the last dregs of the extractor.

During bad weather, winter, generally speaking, visits by relations had to be deflected by other means. Even Father desisted from removing the tops from the beehives when they were covered in snow. Luckily Uncle Keith and Aunt Alice did not visit during the cold season. Unlike Uncle Ted and Aunt Betty from Shropshire.

Uncle Ted, Mother's brother, was a bucolic cattle auctioneer. His wife, a bespectacled midget, kept a small milliner's shop in Telford. Her demure appearance was deceptive. Had she not enjoyed her husband's coarse bellow and vulgar quips, she would never have married him. I'm afraid Uncle Ted's rustic rhymes — delivered in what he considered to be entertaining dialect form — were not favourably received by Father, especially on a freezing winter's day.

> There were an old ram from Wrekin
> As 'ad a curious trick
> Ajumpin over hayricks
> And landin' on his —.
> If yur doan't believe oi

> And think oi be telling a lie
> Just ask the folk at Wrekin
> They'll tell ee same as oi.

Nothing Father tried, not even his pointed endeavour to turn the watering-can in Uncle Ted's direction, ever stifled a second verse.

> Now this auld ram from Wrekin
> They buried im at St Pauls,
> It took three men an' a donkey cart
> To carry away his —.
> If yur doant believe oi
> And think oi tell a lie
> Just ask the folk at Wrekin
> They'll tell ee same as oi.

Dead silence followed the performance.

'Know that one, George?' roared Uncle Ted, slapping Father's rigid back. Father stalked into the conservatory once again. To no avail. Uncle Ted had the unfortunate habit of following him everywhere. He did not seem to appreciate that the reason Father was watering his cactus in the conservatory, for the fourth time that afternoon, was in order to get away from the dreadful intruder.

Mother's innocence was proverbial and she had never even heard of the rude rhyming words so pointedly left unsung in Uncle Ted's refrain. However she sensed that the occasion was not exactly going with a swing, and hastily took both relatives into the drawing-room where they were given tea and eventually got rid of.

'You do realise that brother of yours was drunk, do you Clara?' Father raged after their departure.

'Whatever makes you think that, dear?'

'His breath, woman, didn't you smell his breath?'

'I'm sure Ted doesn't drink, George,' Mother insisted.

'He took the pledge when he was a boy, like the rest of us.'

'It must have been a pledge to support the publicans of Telford for the rest of their lives,' Father declared, before putting on his overcoat and leaving for the shop.

For some reason it was the visits of those of our kin who were blatantly hale and hearty that most upset him. Uncle Ted was one, Uncle Bert was another.

Uncle Bert was a railway engineer from Oswestry who had married Father's elder sister, Kate. 'That Mr Ellis,' Edith would say, 'he's like a man half his age.'

Her remark invariably drove Father into a paroxysm of fury. The trouble was that Uncle Bert could not resist the temptation to show off his physical fitness.

'Don't need the ladder, thank you, George,' he would say, leaping nimbly down from the catwalk on the west wing of the pigeon lofts. Worse still, from Father's point of view, Bert was good with his hands. Father's attempt to pin up the trailing vine in the conservatory necessarily met with disaster. After much violent hammering, the staple would fly out, narrowly missing the visitor's left ear.

'Leave it to me, George,' Uncle Bert would intervene. 'It's the way you bring back the hammer that matters.'

Within minutes the vine was neatly in place.

'There you are, George. It's just a knack.'

It was Uncle Bert who, despite Father's discouragement, resurrected the motor mower. This machine, one of the earliest models, had been relegated for a long time to an empty potting shed. Father much preferred to see the use of a simpler machine for cutting grass, the kind that had to be pushed by hand and therefore required the maximum physical effort on the part of the user. The mechanically assisted contraption remained slumped upon its side between the floorboards of the shed.

'I'll have that working for you in next to no time,' Uncle

Bert insisted. He was as good as his word. After much tinkering with the carburettor, the pistons sprang into life.

'Can't see what my sister ever saw in the man,' Father complained as Bert jumped up with a wave of triumph. 'He's too clever by half, Clara.'

Uncle Bert had only just begun to demonstrate his prowess with the motor mower when, to Father's delight, the throttle stuck. The machine swung into the rockery, totally out of control, carrying Uncle Bert with it.

'You'll need plenty of iodine in that, Bert,' Father said, as the wounded engineer rolled up his trouser leg.

'Steady on there, George. This stuff stings.'

I don't remember ever seeing Father chuckle before. A memorable sight in itself, the experience was so unusual that his top dentures fell out.

Father was toying with the idea of applying a completely unnecessary tourniquet to Uncle Bert's calf, but finally resisted the impulse. Instead he managed to entangle his victim in a complex way of bandages, rather like a spider securing a fly.

'That should stop him calling for a bit, Clara,' Father observed, as the visitor drove stiffly away on his Norton motorbike, with Aunt Kate clinging on behind.

I suppose the reason that health and vigour in his kinsfolk particularly exasperated Father was because he was a pharmacist. He felt more at home with sickness and disease. Certainly I noticed he was far less hostile to those relations who arrived at Resthaven afflicted with some gratifying complaint.

'Hope for the best, prepare for the worst.'

While constantly quoting this motto, Father acted only on the second half. He made the fullest arrangements for ultimate catastrophe of every kind, but would have nothing to do with hope.

'That's in order, then,' he said, opening his luncheon

bottle of ginger beer. He had returned from the shop three minutes earlier than usual. This was because his cousin Maud was due to arrive. She was recovering from an operation and Mother had rashly invited her to Resthaven for convalescence.

'What's that dear?'

'I've just visited Mrs Jennings in Vernon Street, on my way home,' said Father. 'She's agreed to lay Maud out. She can't last long in her condition. It's best to look ahead.'

Cousin Maud lived to be eighty, in fact, outdoing Father by a whole twelve months. At Maud's funeral, Mother was heard to say, greatly daring, 'Your father wasn't always right when he looked ahead, was he?'

CHAPTER 13

CHRISTMAS CHEER

Christmas comes but once a year
And when it comes it brings good cheer.

Father was quick to remind us of the truth of the first line
of this adage. Where he tended to waver was over the
second. It was not that he approached the festive season
in the manner of Scrooge. On the contrary, he conscien-
tiously willed himself into a semblance of Yuletide Spirit.
His problem was to sustain this unfamiliar role for more
than an hour at a time.

In principle, for instance, he had no objection to carol
singers. Except, that is to say, 'when they try my patience,
Clara.'

This, I'm afraid, is what they usually did.

'Leave them to me,' he would call out to Edith in the
kitchen.

Trumpeting indignantly into a large white handkerchief, taken out of his cuff, he emerged from the dining-
room into the hall. The Victorian iron knocker on the front
door was thudding away for the seventh time. I watched,
from behind the umbrella stand, as he flung open the
door. An icy wind gushed in, bringing down the sprig of
holly — a piece without berries — which Father had stuck
between the antlers of the stag's head shot in Wynnstay
Park.

'Caught!' he snapped at the nearest urchin, shivering
in the jagged shadow of the monkey-puzzle tree, with the
street lamp behind him.

The unfortunate child had never encountered anything like Father before.

'And now that I've got you,' he went on 'let me hear Good King Wenceslas right through from beginning to end.'

'But we only know the first verse, mister.'

Father's glare was terrible to behold.

'Edith,' he roared. 'Bring the hymn book.'

'Run for it, Gerry,' called the other boy.

Father slammed the door upon the retreating duo.

'If a job's worth doing, it's worth doing well,' he fulminated, returning to his nasal syringe by the coke fire.

I darted back into the kitchen, where Aunty Carrie was helping Edith with the Christmas cooking.

'Phew' she exclaimed, 'he's always been the same. Ever since he came into the district. Putting the fear of God into folk.' She cut open the wax paper on a jar of mincemeat. 'People used to walk into his chemist's shop just to gawp at him.'

'Why was that?' I asked. She picked up the rolling-pin.

'Have you seen a picture of one of them Zulus?'

I certainly had. My *Boys' Own Annual* was full of illustrations of gigantic warriors descending on brave British soldiers in the Zulu War, their spears poised at the ready, huge heads thrown back.

'Well you know the way they wear their hair,' Aunty Carrie continued, 'all stuck up on end?'

'With mud,' I interrupted 'to frighten their enemies?'

'Well I don't know about enemies, but your father scared the living daylights out of my sister Brenda.'

Father's hair was still rather startling, very thick and fuzzy, but now beginning to grey a little.

'Was it black, then?' I asked.

'No, bright ginger,' said Aunty Carrie. She scattered a handful of flour on the pastry board.

'As well as his hair, you see, your father was that tall

in his great black morning coat, like the undertaker. And his eyes bored right through your head as he fired questions at you like bullets.'

Aunty Carrie helped Edith tie a white cloth around the plum pudding basin with a piece of string.

'Before your father took over the chemist's shop, our Brenda used to buy a regular two-penn'oth of Fisherman's Friend cough sweets there. Once she come up against Mr Knox Mawer, she wouldn't go near the place. She changed to aniseed balls from Mrs Scott, the paper shop.'

Other people, including my friends, commented on Father's appearance.

'This,' Donald Rathwell used to say, 'is how he walks down Grosvenor Road.'

Donald threw back his head and stalked forward with cheeks puffed out. I blushed in fury and attempted a feeble counter-imitation of Mr Rathwell in his plus-fours. I was unwilling to concede that Father was different from other fathers.

At that time neither Donald nor I had tumbled to the secret of Santa Claus. However, I do remember being a little puzzled as to why the red gowned gentleman in a sleigh, who visited my particular bedside on Christmas Eve, left behind a surgical stocking, stuffed with nail-brushes, combs, sticking plaster, and a strange board game known as 'Gibbs Giant Decay', given away with the Christmas tube of toothpaste.

Another parental difference was that Mr Rathwell had turkey for Christmas dinner, while Father had goose, no doubt preferring the richer flavour. At precisely one p.m. on Christmas Day, Father took his place in the carving chair. Mother perched at the other end of the table, hoping, without much confidence, that the meal might go smoothly for once in a while. We four children sat in our allotted places, waiting for Grace.

'Constance Mary,' came the sharp directive from on

high. My second sister's correct name was Mary Constance, but Father never got it quite right.

'For what we are about to receive, may the Lord make us truly thankful,' she mumbled.

'Amen,' Father added sharply.

Edith brought in the goose. Mother had already set out the other dishes.

'These serving plates, Clara,' Father observed, 'they're barely warm. Won't do, you know.'

The barely warm plates were handed down the table, in total silence, each bearing a portion of goose. The contents of the other dishes were ladled out. We waited for Father to pick up his knife and fork, then followed suit. Father ate at a gallop — the leg of goose, the half-breast, the stuffing, the five potatoes (two roast, two steamed, one baked), the three portions of vegetables (cabbage, mashed turnip, brussels sprouts), the apple sauce, and the very thick gravy.

Immediately upon clearing his plate, Father turned to the bottle and opener set alongside his silver napkin-ring in strict formation. Within seconds he downed an immense glass of Stone ginger beer, without pausing for breath. The volcanic hiccups which followed were pitched in a strangely high register, like his speaking voice. It reminded me of the sound made by my old teddy bear when pressed in the stomach. No one was permitted to refer in any way to Father's performance, even though it lasted several minutes. All heads had to be kept discreetly lowered until it was over.

'This custard, Clara. Far too lumpy. She'll have to go.' The reference was to Edith who had brought in the sauce bowl along with the plum pudding.

'But I made it, dear.'

'Humph.'

After the plum pudding, Father solemnly pulled a cracker with my eldest sister, Evelyn. He even insisted upon donning a brown paper hat, much to everybody's embarrassment. It had split up the back, being far too small for him, and was now perched forward, giving the effect of an army forage cap. This was somehow appropriate for the military-style operations that followed.

'Edith! Dessert!' Father called. 'I'll try the walnuts to begin with.'

Bits of shell began to fly in all directions as Father operated the adjustable pincers of the Sheffield-steel walnut-crackers, supplied by Edith. After the opening barrage, a comparative quiet fell on no-man's land. From our slit-trenches on either side we children peered across the expanse of white cloth, as he munched his way through the edible debris in front of him.

'You four can take on the hazels,' he instructed us. We were each issued with a mini pair of nutcrackers for the purpose.

'Can't see any brazils in the dish, Clara,' Father said. Mother sprang to the sideboard for the missing nuts, especially large ones from the grocery shop of Worshipful Brother Dutton.

The brazils presented a special challenge.

'Where is the Royal Windsor?' he demanded. This sophisticated piece of weaponry — the Royal Windsor All-Purpose Nutvendor (patent pending) — had been handed down from the captain's table on the SS *Acacia*, Grandfather's ship. It was kept in a silk-lined case along with the fish knives in the dining-room cabinet, third drawer down. By means of the giant clamp on the Windsor, Father exploded a rapid succession of brazils. This time the noise was deafening as more shrapnel ricocheted everywhere. When Father finally rose from the table, it took Edith a good five minutes with the brass-handled soft brush and brass tray to clear away.

The carnage of the Great Nut Offensive was the grand

climax of the whole dinner. One more solemn rite remained — the wireless broadcast by King George.

'Edith! The King.'

From the urgency of Father's summons, it always seemed to me that His Majesty was unable to address his Empire until Edith was in the room, sitting bolt upright on the oak chair in the draught by the door. Listening with Father to the King's Speech was like taking communion. Father did not actually require us to kneel, although the enormous wireless set, around which we sat in a half-circle, closely resembled a shrine. Frowning down from the topmost pinnacle was the loudspeaker. This was shaped like a church window, except that instead of stained glass there was set in the fretwork arch a mysterious piece of steel gauze.

The bottom tier of the edifice consisted of a walnut cabinet with long spindly legs and two little cupboard doors which kept swinging open unless wedged with pieces of the *Radio Times*. This was the *sanctum sanctorum* where Father kept the wet and dry batteries. In between the two tiers was what was laughingly described as the receiver, an illuminated window painted with strange names like Hilversum, Bucharest and Amsterdam.

Not that I am suggesting that Father laughed. Entirely the reverse. With an air of the utmost solemnity, he would bend to adjust the various knobs and dials which were to transmit the Royal message.

The moment when the King's voice came through had the pure thrill of the miraculous. It sounded startlingly clear.

'Through one of the marvels of modern science,' His Majesty began, 'I am enabled this Christmas Day to speak to all my peoples throughout the Empire. I take it as a good omen that wireless should have reached its present perfection at a time when the Empire has been linked in closer union. For it offers us immense possibilities to make that union closer still.'

Here Father nodded encouragingly towards our own wireless set which was certainly doing its best to achieve the required standard of perfection.

'It may be,' His Majesty went on, 'that our future will lay upon us more than one stern test.' Father leaned forward. Stern tests were just his line.

'Our past will have taught us how to meet it unshaken,' continued King George. 'For the present the work to which we are equally bound is to arrive at a reasoned tranquillity within our borders, to regain prosperity without self-seeking, and to carry with us those whom the burden of past years has disheartened or overborne. I speak to you now from my home and from my heart to you all. To each I wish a Happy Christmas. God bless you all.'

'And God bless you, sir,' said Father, addressing the exhausted valves. He was rather pink with emotion. 'Just the message I would have delivered myself.' He turned to my eldest sister. 'I hope you've got it all down, Evelyn.' She had been delegated to keep a short-hand note.

Evelyn peered short-sightedly at the scribbles on her page. 'Yes, Father,' she said. He rose to his feet which was the signal that the Ritual was concluded.

'I've lit the fire in the drawing-room, Mr Knox Mawer,' said Edith, her short rest also over. She was carrying an enormous bucket of coke and a large box of matches. Father moved out into the hall, humming tunelessly like a giant bluebottle, an indication that he was momentarily satisfied with life.

'Tell those children, Clara,' he called, before closing the drawing-room door, 'that I am not to be disturbed.'

That was the time when we read our Christmas annuals in the dining-room, poring over pictures of jolly families lounging on modern three-piece suites, with fathers in cheerful pullovers, making jokes to mothers who all had marcel waves and looked like Myrna Loy.

Two hours later, the bell at the side door rang.

'Colonel and Mrs Jarvis Roberts' Edith announced. The Jarvis Robertses, who lived in Grove Row, the street behind Grosvenor Road, never failed to arrive punctually at six p.m. Naturally this annual social event had its roots in Freemasonry. I studied with keen interest the special Masonic grip applied by the Colonel to Father's outstretched hand as Edith ushered the visitors into the drawing-room.

Mr Jarvis Roberts was a Colonel in the Territorials, but despite his impressive military moustache, of lesser Masonic rank than Father. Mrs Jarvis Roberts was larger than the Colonel, and quite pleased with him except for his lesser Masonic rank.

As an experienced infantryman the Colonel insisted upon taking the shortest route to Resthaven from Grove Row, which meant coming through our back garden. Unfortunately Father treated himself to a special Christmas Box every year, to be trenched into the herbaceous border by 'volunteers' during the holiday week, Boxing Day to New Year. This took the unsightly form of a cartload of fresh manure upended by Worshipful Brother Bowman, of Wynnstay Farm, on the previous afternoon, inside our back gates. However skilfully the Jarvis Robertses sought to negotiate this hazard, they inevitably brought in with them the tang of the farmyard.

It was Father's custom to pass Christmas evening with his favourite word game, played with cards, known as Kan-U-Go, which had been introduced to teach us how to spell correctly. So far as the unfortunate Jarvis Robertses were concerned, despite the passage of several hours, they certainly could not go — either home or anywhere else. Even fortified with ham sandwiches and shop sherry, they wilted visibly, while the strange smell expanded, in the airless drawing-room. It was still there when I helped Edith with the tidying up next morning. I suppose other people associate Christmas with the festive scent of plum pudding, turkey, and mince pies. For me, I'm afraid, it was always Worshipful Brother Bowman's farmyard manure.

CHAPTER 14

THE AUGUST HOLIDAY

It was not unusual for Father's August holiday to begin with a loud explosion in the kitchen. Whenever he meddled with the filling of hot thermos flasks of tea, one or other of them seemed destined to slip out of his hand. And since no notice could be taken of any accident for which Father was responsible, the rest of us had to crunch our way through the scattered silver fragments with averted eyes.

'Move along there,' Father called, speeding us on our way.

Outside in the garage, a hearse-like car, especially hired for the journey, was piled high with the several trunks and cases Father considered essential for a visit to what he called the Cornish Riviera.

His choice of venue was entirely dictated by the weather statistics published in *The Times*. For several weeks beforehand, he marked these out in red, with one of his battery of coloured propelling pencils.

'Cornwall has it again, Clara,' he announced to Mother over his steel-rimmed reading spectacles. He went through the identical procedure every year with exactly the same result.

'Precisely 3.4 per cent above the sunshine average,' came the declaration at the end of his calculations.

'The change will do us good, dear, wherever we go and whatever the weather,' Mother said.

'You're quite wrong,' she was told.

Father swung round in his chair and glared at me and my three sisters.

'Just look at these children of yours, Clara,' he said. 'Nothing but a natural dose of Vitamin D will put any sort of energy into them! Only obtainable I'm afraid from the hottest rays of the sun. We'll have them lolling about the place until they go back to school if something isn't done about it.'

Any house less equipped for lolling about than Resthaven was hard to imagine. Father loathed the very term easy chair, and as for sofas, they were complete anathema. The new word 'lounge' was particularly condemned. Nothing but drawing-room would do, although this term had overtones of elegance inapplicable to our spartan decor of dark brown paint and threadbare carpeting. Perhaps the garden was the place Father had in mind for our mythical state of idleness. I tried in vain to imagine myself lolling about Father's horticultural barrack square of regimented borders and ranks of corrugated iron outhouses.

There was certainly no question of lolling about in the back of the hired car. From the moment we ricocheted out into Grosvenor Road, Father's driving had us tense and upright and clinging desperately to the straps.

'He's gone as white as a sheet, George,' Mother reported, only five minutes later. By then Father was hurtling alongside the lake at Ellesmere into the neighbouring county of Shropshire.

'Perhaps you ought to stop for him.'

'No point in pandering to the child,' Father called above the clash of gears. 'If I halt now he'll never find his sea-legs.'

Whatever these strange things might be, I hoped they would turn up soon. Fortunately, just outside Shrewsbury, a steep hill, combined with Father's manic use of the throttle, never failed to cause the motor to overheat and so rescue me from disaster.

'An absolute disgrace,' Father complained, quite unaware of the extent of his maltreatment of the internal combustion engine. Amidst a cloud of steam he was forced to draw into a layby. There, the bilious prisoner was granted five minutes' remission to walk about in the fresh air.

'Remind me never to take a car from young Boot again, Clara,' Father said.

Young Boot, the proprietor of Wrexham Car Hire Ltd, struck me as a man of immense age, with his bald head and white beard, but Mother explained that was what he had always been called since taking over the firm from his uncle, Old Boot.

When the time came to set off once more, new seating directions were issued. Father turned to my second sister, a chubby girl with a dark fringe and a fixed expression of trepidation on her face.

'Constance Mary,' he said, 'I want you to change places with your mother. I need a map reader from now on and you seem to be the sole member of the family with any knowledge whatsoever of geography.' He handed her the familiar leather-bound Collins *Route Map of the British Isles*.

'Not that there isn't considerable room for improvement in the subject, judging from your last school report.'

Father had a pathological dread of bestowing unqualified praise.

With Mother perched uneasily between the rest of us, Father unleashed the hand-brake and we roared off again into the pouring rain. To me, the squelch of the primitive windscreen wiper was like some relentless metronome measuring the endless minutes to the next stop at Hereford.

'Quick sharp there, Constance Mary,' Father called. 'Which turn is it here for Kidderminster, right or left?'

'I'm not sure, Father,' she said peering anxiously through her misted-up glasses at the atlas on her lap.

'Hurry up, girl, for heaven's sake.'

'Right,' she squeaked.

Father shot out a large gauntleted hand through the flap by the driving wheel, causing the driver of a large Humber immediately behind to screech to a halt against our bumper.

'What on earth are you doing?' came the muffled voice of the driver.

'Teaching you a lesson in road manners, that's what I'm doing,' Father shouted in reply. 'Learn to keep your distance!'

The presence of a single other vehicle on the road he was using was enough for Father.

'B roads from now on, Constance Mary,' he instructed.

This decree was the knell of doom from my point of view. It meant that we got no further than Gloucestershire on the first day.

For our overnight accommodation, Father stuck rigidly to the bed and breakfast guide issued by the Ramblers' Association, entitled *Bright and Cheery Up Betimes*. On one occasion the guide landed us in Stonehampton at the whitewashed Travellers' Rest, bright and cheery but not exactly restful. We were treated to an all-night session, from the tap-room downstairs, of 1914–18 choruses still popular fifteen years on.

> 'Pack up your troubles in your auld kit-bag
> And smoile, smoile, smoile.'

Father declined to do either of these things. He also refused to pay the bill, on the ground that the inn-keeper had 'No licence for musical entertainment of any kind.'

Our progress through Devon, the following day, was somewhat hampered by Father's strange addiction to Devonshire clotted cream. This was ordered with porridge at a late breakfast in Exeter, with pudding at lunchtime, and with strawberry jam scones at tea.

As a kind of atonement for this period of gross indulgence, Father made a point of driving us to view His Majesty's Prison on Dartmoor. This involved a detour, but he considered an important moral message was called for.

'No Devonshire clotted cream served in there,' he warned, as we gazed up at the dismal grey stone penitentiary. He looked down at me. 'And this is precisely where you could end up if you take the wrong turning.'

I hoped this was not a reference to my inability to read a map.

'Poor men,' Mother sighed.

'Poor men indeed,' Father agreed. 'Yet each one of those unfortunate inmates began life like these children with freedom of choice — the upward path of honest endeavour or the downward track of sloth and crime.'

We looked at each other uneasily.

'Now can that boy read the inscription over the entrance?' he asked. The atmosphere was so forbidding that I was reluctant to raise my eyes at all.

'Abandon hope all ye who enter here,' Father recited solemnly.

Appropriately chastened, I followed the family back into the car. It would not have surprised me to read, one day, the same message above the glass door leading into Father's office at the shop.

After another fraught interval, 'circumventing Bodmin', as Father put it, we pulled up at our destination, Atlantic View, Newquay. This was a semi-detached temperance hotel in one of the side streets of the town. The name was something of a misnomer. Standing in the front porch, Father was the only one of us tall enough actually to glimpse the postage stamp view of the sea through the intervening houses, but he was able to describe it to us in no uncertain fashion.

'Those breakers should do something to stir up their sluggish systems tomorrow, Clara,' he declared, as we struggled past him with the luggage.

He had, as usual, timed our arrival to coincide with the evening meal.

'Boiled mackeral for six, is it, Mr Knox Mawer?' asked the proprietress, when he checked in. Her visitors' book had a column for nationality, consisting of endless ditto marks under the heading BRITISH. Father made a point of writing Welsh.

'Wales is my adopted country,' he used to explain. A mixed blessing for the Welsh, it might be thought, although Father was unswerving in his determination to uphold the cause of all things relating to the Principality.

'Mark you,' he inevitably added by way of a rare quip, 'I haven't brought my harp.'

The proprietress of Atlantic View bore the unusual name of Mrs Earthy, which provoked the other joke made by Father at holiday time. He would take his seat at the head of our allotted table in the alcove, then turn to the other diners.

'You'll find Mrs Earthy dirt cheap,' he would say, with a short, barking laugh.

At least he made sure that she did not overhear this witticism, because he greatly approved of Mrs E, as he called her, a well-scrubbed widow with a shingle. Upon his every visit, she invariably appointed him captain of the Atlantic View beach cricket team.

Apart from beach cricket, energetic salt-water bathing was the only other appointed recreation of which Father approved.

The amusement park, for instance, adjoining the Hotel Atlantic, was invariably given, in Father's term, a wide berth. On one occasion, however, his scientific curiosity was aroused by the sight of a billboard outside the entrance. 'PROFESSOR DAREWSKI'S BAVARIAN FLEA CIRCUS.'

The white-bearded proprietor was seated alongside selling tickets. Father stopped in his tracks. 'How is it done, Professor?' he demanded in the extra-loud voice necessary for foreigners.

'They vork mit zee vires,' explained the owner enthusiastically. 'Vy not kom unt zee?'

I was standing with my face pressed to the turnstile, my attention fixed on the booth selling candy floss — 'sugar filth' in Father's words.

'Zay dance unt ballet, fight mit swords and valk zee tight rope,' the professor persisted, 'a vunderful cheap show for zee family.'

Not surprisingly Father was unwilling to fork out for six tickets.

'I'll take your word for it, professor,' he assured him, shepherding us away.

The encounter put Father in a reflective mood.

'Another example of the mind of the Great Geometrician, Clara,' he declared over lunch. 'No matter how lowly, for all creatures the message is clear.'

He glanced up at me and gave the sharp bark that heralded one of his jokes.

'This boy has much in common with the flea. Generally an irritant but can be taught to be useful!'

Apart from that exceptional foray, the sea was the focal point of the holiday programme. On our first morning in Newquay, he booked himself a changing hut on the South Front. He alone was allowed to use it, to change into his wasp bathing costume and black rubber cap. The rest of us (Mother did not swim) had to go down ready clad for the breakers.

Aside from his swimming dress, Father's changing was restricted to a yellowing flannel shirt and the beach footwear. In the dank privacy of the hut, Father would remove his polished black boots and put on an enormous pair of brown sandals.

The only sandals I had ever seen resembling Father's were those worn by Moses in front of the burning bush — the ones that he was removing at God's command. I knew then well because the scene was depicted in the biblical print hanging on the upstairs landing just outside my bedroom door at Resthaven.

Sometimes I used to imagine that one day God might order Father to remove *his* sandals. Perhaps it was a good thing, in that eventuality, that he always kept on his heather-mixture woollen stockings underneath — the ones knitted for him upon Aunty Carrie's sock machine. The thought of Father conversing with God, in his bare feet — like Moses — was unthinkable.

Apart from the Moses sandals, and flannel shirt, Father made no concession to beachwear. He supervised our health-giving activities from a large deck-chair, clad in a formal three-piece suit.

'Why not do without the waistcoat, dear?' Mother suggested one particularly scorching afternoon.

'You surely don't expect me to display my braces, Clara!' he replied.

The subject was not mentioned again.

Father's hiring of a personal changing hut impressed me as a lavish touch. Moreover I had once seen, in his wallet, the astonishing vision of a white five pound note. I assumed therefore that he must secretly be quite rich. It is difficult to understand how I sustained this fantasy in the face of Mother's household frugality, the patches on my trousers, and the handing down from sister to sister of outgrown gymslips. The spartan nature of our accommodation at Atlantic View hardly suggested a deep parental pocket. Father's Kan-U-Go sessions, for instance, had to be played out upon a faded green baize card table set up by Mrs Earthy in the cramped conditions of the residents' sitting-room. This was wedged between the badly stained gate-leg table in the centre of the room and the frayed window seat.

'If that boy would only move his chair right up against the coal scuttle, Clara,' Father would complain 'he won't be inconveniencing nurse Moult at her sampler.'

Miss Moult, a retired nursing sister with a stiff back, was one of Mrs Earthy's permanent residents. The nurse was never seen to wear anything but black alpaca, and from her grim demeanour I assumed her to be permanently in mourning for her unfortunate patients.

'Why can't that boy sit on the arm of your sofa, Clara,' was another of Father's demands, 'there's no way Mr and Mrs Vanderoost can sort out their stamp collection on the gate-leg table while his head is in their way.'

Mr and Mrs Vanderoost were, as their name suggests, of Flemish origin. They looked strangely alike, both round and pasty. The couple owned a stable of donkeys — subcontracted to the Newquay Deck Chair Company — and then lived at Atlantic View off the meagre proceeds. How they came to be staying there in the first place remained a mystery. Perhaps they were refugees from the German invasion of Flanders in 1914.

'Dos is goot,' was all Mr Vanderoost ever said as I abandoned the chair by the table to comply with Father's decree.

By that stage of the holiday it was vital to obey Father's commands with even greater alacrity than usual. Despite the protection of his large grey trilby, worn with the brim turned down all round, Father's nose had become badly burned from the sun on the South Beach. This made his temper even shorter than usual, despite the application of several bottles of calamine lotion, the contents of which dried up in useless pink rivulets down either side of the stricken protruberance.

'Are you sure your nose isn't too sore for you to go out

with the cricket team this year, Mr Mawer?' Mrs Earthy inquired.

'A good captain never leaves the bridge, Mrs E,' he insisted. Like the reference to my sea-legs, this was no doubt another subconscious reversion to his nautical ancestry.

Father's cricket team consisted of himself and us four children. Mother was never invited to participate. In addition there were Mr and Mrs Vanderoost, Miss Moult, who surprisingly kept wicket, Mrs Earthy, our pace bowler, and the hotel's domestic staff of two. The latter comprised our opening bats — Godfrey, a simple minded Cornishman with rosy cheeks and Ena, the overworked cook, who had a permanent cold and was constantly wheezing up and down the narrow stairs of Atlantic View with jugs of hot water for the wash bowls in the bedrooms.

Our opponents in the cricket fixture, the inhabitants of Wavecrest, the private hotel next door, were insufferably proud of their single AA star.

'There's been some double-dealing to earn them that,' Father maintained, 'and that No Vacancies sign of theirs is pure window dressing. It's as much as they can do to field a cricket team.'

This was true, but their captain, Mr Bumphrey, a retired bank manager, seemed to have the maddening knack of always winning the toss. He never failed to put us into bat, especially if there was a wind blowing from under the pier to whip the sand up into our faces.

In his own opinion Father shone at fielding in the slips, and provided he held a catch, which he usually managed to do from off a wildly hitting lady batsman in the Wave-crest team, he remained in even spirits. So far as I remember, we lost every fixture, but provided Father had 'picked one out of the air' — his phrase — he bought an ice-cream for every member of both teams. Unfortunately he was never able to avoid a *contretemps* with the Italian ice-cream vendor.

'You've been putting custard powder in this mixture again,' Father told him. 'I'll denounce you to the health authorities, mark my words.'

We retreated to our respective hotels in the wake of a stream of Italian curses.

'Ignore the fellow,' Father instructed. 'Remember he's a foreigner.'

The Holiday Mood, like the Christmas Spirit, was something he found difficult to sustain. From his point of view, therefore, Sunday morning church made a welcome break in the hectic round of seaside frivolities.

'This year we'll try St Mary's,' he announced, 'instead of the parish church.'

Mrs Earthy was dubious. 'St Mary's is rather high, Mr Mawer,' she warned.

Mystified, I prepared myself for a stiff climb in my uncomfortable Sunday shoes, and was relieved to find us walking downhill to St Mary's, which turned out to be on the harbour side of the town.

Proceedings had barely started when puffs of oddly scented smoke began to surface around the altar, along with a persistent tinkling sound rather like Mrs Earthy's dinner bell. Through the corner of my eye I could see Father's neck — always a barometer of his mood — deepen to crimson.

'That's more than enough, Clara,' he hissed to Mother, before we had even got as far as the prayers. Under the cover of the opening hymn Mother ushered us outside.

'Brazen popery, brazen popery,' Father kept repeating as we made our way back to Atlantic View. Our motor car was already packed for instant departure. Father gave the starting handle an angry turn. The engine roared into life.

'Why don't I ask Mrs Earthy to make you a nice mug

of Horlicks?' Mother suggested. 'You'll feel much calmer for the journey.'

'I don't want to feel calmer,' Father replied. With the adrenalin of religious intolerance still coursing happily through his veins, Father set forth upon what he called the return trip. This involved a manic safari of cathedrals, abbeys, castles, and ancient monuments of every size, shape and description.

'Are these children taking it all in, Clara, that's what I want to know?' he demanded as we tramped the length and breadth of Glastonbury Abbey, scaled the craggy slope of St Michaels Mount, panted up the winding stone steps to the bell tower of Gloucester Cathedral, and traversed acres of medieval crypts and cloisters. Not unexpectedly, Father himself became increasingly peevish as the marathon proceeded.

'Why is the boy falling behind again, Clara?'

'I expect he's tired dear.'

'Tell him to stop that awful whistling sound he keeps making through that stupid gap in his front teeth.'

'Just a little habit, George. I'm sure he'll grow out of it.'

'Why are his stockings always rucked around his ankles?'

'They do slip down easily, you know, especially with his skinny legs.'

'Tell him to move back from the edge there, does he want to break his neck?'

Mother beckoned me down.

'Have another egg, George,' she said.

Father took out the last of the hard-boiled eggs, fortifying himself for a final brass-rubbing session in Ellesmere Parish Church.

As we turned at last into Grosvenor Road, Wrexham, we were all of us, including Mother, fast asleep. Except for Father, ever wakeful at the wheel.

However one more trauma lay ahead, heralded by a particularly alarming cry of rage from our zealous driver.

'By thunder, Clara, they've done it again!'

Father flung open his driving door and sprang onto the pavement by Number 26.

'Done what dear?'

'You know perfectly well, what!'

He pointed a quivering finger at the evergreen which hung over our garden gate, now considerably reduced in size. We walked past and followed Father in a straggling procession to the front door of Resthaven. There was a familiar looking notice pinned to it, bearing the coat-of-arms of the Wrexham Corporation.

'Pursuant to the Road Safety Byelaws 1921 Section 97 (b),' he read out, 'the Corporation has authorised the removal of the coniferous growth obtruding from this property over the highway.'

Mother shook her head in sympathy.

'Bureaucratic barbarians,' Father exclaimed.

Unfortunately, much the same thing happened every year. The council workmen took advantage of Father's absence on the August holiday to carry out in peace all necessary lopping operations.

'Last year my sycamore,' Father bewailed, 'the year before my beech, and now they've ruined the finest monkey-puzzle tree in North Wales. I've a good mind not to go away at all next year. That would fox them.'

'And I could always take the children to cousin Hetty's at Morecambe,' Mother said, in the meekest of voices.

We hardly dared look at one another. The prospect of such a freedom was altogether too intoxicating.

'Anyway,' he said, before disappearing into the dining-room for the evening news bulletin and his glass of ginger beer, 'these children can set about carrying the logs down below. There's still a good half-hour before the light goes.'

For the time being, life had returned to normal at Resthaven.

CHAPTER 15

FATHER AND THE ENTENTE CORDIALE

It was Whit Monday 1935. According to the *Daily Mail*, mankind was in turmoil everywhere.

'Civil disturbances spread throughout India,' Father intoned, taking his customary seat in the breakfast room.

'Tribesmen blow up railway in Palestine.'

A sound like a whiplash made us all jump as Father turned over to the second page. Apparently there was trouble in London too.

'Mosely's blackshirts run amok,' he informed us mysteriously, 'Strikes me the world is falling into complete anarchy.'

We maintained the usual respectful silence while Father attacked his breakfast grapefruit. In Resthaven, at least, authority reigned supreme.

'I don't like the sound of it, Clara,' he said, dismembering the final segment.

'No dear,' Mother agreed.

Father was not however referring to the headlines in the *Daily Mail*. He had turned his attention to something far more disturbing which had landed in the table with the morning post.

'Just look at this.'

He tapped his thumb nail on the first paragraph of a neatly handwritten letter.

'This fool idea from Miss Davies of a student exchange scheme. Can't think why she expects my support!'

Miss Davies was my eldest sister's French teacher, at Grove Park Grammar School.

'Evelyn says it's the only way to make sure of getting a distinction, George,' Mother explained.

'The only way,' he snapped. 'What about work?'

As Evelyn made a hasty retreat with the porridge plates, Mother was handed the letter.

'It doesn't look as though it will cost much, dear,' she said. 'The French girl will have Evelyn to stay at her home to learn her language. In return we'll have the child back with us.'

'Why does it have to be France?' he complained 'the most decadent country in Europe.'

'French happens to be the language Evelyn is studying, George,' Mother pointed out.

Father was now handling the final item in the morning post — his weekly *Pharmaceutical Journal*. With a warning gesture he held up the back cover — an advertisement in bold letters for Jeyes Fluid.

'This is what they need Over There,' he said. For a moment the rest of us were puzzled.

'Have I never told you about the state of the public conveniences in the French capital?'

It was the only thing Father had told us about Paris, which he had visited in the spring of 1920.

Far from being a romantic assignment he had been obliged to dash across the channel 'to rescue your Aunt Kate and Aunt Carol'. His sisters, then in their early thirties, had lost their money on the Metro, somewhere between Napoleon's Tomb — 'highly over-rated' and the Eiffel Tower — 'totally pointless so far as I could see'.

'But I won't be going to Paris, Father,' Evelyn ventured. She nervously pushed aside a strand of hair from her forehead. 'I'm to go to a chateau in the country. It's got a vineyard where they produce a famous brand of wine.'

This piece of information reminded Father of something

upon his own estate that needed prompt attention. Within
seconds all four of us were trailing in his wake to the
conservatory for what he called 'a small team effort'. The
central stem of his grapevine, which normally drooped
across the glass dome, had broken loose from the moor-
ing. Its purple leaves were now entangled with the row
of cactus plants on the underlying shelf. There seemed to
be six very small grapes hanging from one end, seven,
when I looked harder. After hearing Evelyn speak of the
chateau in France, I was rashly carried away by
enthusiasm.

'Perhaps we could make some wine here, Father.'

He glared back at me.

'Like you have in the shop,' I tried again. 'Er,
Wincarnis.'

There was another silence.

'Or even communion wine,' I faltered, adjusting my
suggestion to Father's view of life.

Without removing his basilisk stare from me, Father
unwound a long length of twine from the pocket of his
gardening apron. For a moment I thought I was going to
be hung up, for insubordination.

'Those,' he remarked coldly, 'are dessert grapes — for
table-consumption only.'

I could never remember seeing any upon our table.
Casting my mind back there had been one occasion when
I was dispatched with a token bunch for Mrs Jarvis
Roberts. She was then a patient at the War Memorial
Hospital — something to do with veins, according to
Aunty Carrie.

Meanwhile, Father had turned away to inspect the dam-
aged vine. 'The first thing to do,' he declared, 'is to replace
the supporting nail.' With the assistance of Evelyn and
Constance Mary, the step-ladder was dragged into position. Father climbed up.

'Hammer!' he called down to me.

He was now directly above me, blocking out the light more effectively than the blackest cloud.

'Not the mallet, stupid boy.'

Evelyn quickly passed up the correct tool.

'The secret,' he went on, 'is to bring the head back and strike dead centre.'

With a loud ping, the nail ricocheted into Father's spectacles, cracking a lens. An awful silence fell. It was a serious development, almost a catastrophe.

Claiming that this was my fault 'for not standing still' and that he might have been 'blinded', Father descended, like Zeus from the Heavens. The next day he delegated the task to Mr Humes, the gardener, who restored the plant to its correct position during his two-minute tea-break. Evelyn was told to help brush up the dead vine leaves.

'Your French friends will undoubtedly make the most of free British labour.'

We looked at each other in astonishment. The pronouncement was the first and only indication we had been given that Father had sanctioned the student exchange scheme!

More was to come, however. At the dining-room table that evening Father helped himself to the last slice of cold beetroot before clearing his throat.

'She'll be needing a new gym-slip, Clara,' he said, 'for this trip to France.'

Evelyn's face fell.

'I don't want her letting the side down. Go to C. D. Jones's tomorrow and get the best.'

Mr Christmas Day Jones was the owner of Wrexham's principal drapery store. This centre of Wrexham's *haute couture* occupied a tall mock-Tudor building in Hope Street, with a lethal sprung door, and a large plate glass window occupied by a group of pallid dummies. As a very small boy I imagined them to be relatives of his family, paid to stand still. Then early one morning, on my way to Acton School, I saw them in a shocking state of undress. Propped up in stricken attitudes of mute appeal, I thought they must be victims of some dreadful crime, especially when I caught sight of the headless torso of a lady in a pink corset slumped against the partition. The unmistakable signs of *rigor mortis* had haunted my dreams for many weeks afterwards.

It was the tone of Mother's voice which interrupted my reverie — that rare note which only came when she was summoning up courage to contradict Father.

'What Evelyn really needs, George, is a new frock.'

'Frock!'

It was as though Mother had suggested an evening gown of ostrich feathers like the one Ginger Rogers wore in *Top Hat*.

There was a prolonged silence while Father rolled up his white napkin and threaded it slowly back into his silver christening ring. Whenever I looked at this object, I had a mental picture of Father at his christening — a large purple-faced baby, bawling with fury, fists flailing.

Finally he spoke.

'Well, try to make sure that this "frock" is a size too big for the girl,' Father decreed, 'otherwise you'll find she's grown out of it before you can say Jack Robinson.'

Evelyn was slender and pale, like Mother, rather small for her age. It was hard to think she would grow out of anything. In any case, from what I could see of the stock on display — I was taken along by Mother for a new pair of short flannel trousers — Mr C.D. seemed to specialise in large dresses for the matronly farmers' wives who came into town on market day.

Standing between Mother and Evelyn, I wondered why all the assistants behind the counters were dressed in black. Perhaps it was something to do with the notice on the wall: FUNERAL ORDERS PROMPTLY EXECUTED.

In addition to his lady staff, Mr C.D. enjoyed what he himself described to Mother as 'a useful bit of mechanical assistance'. He had the entire shop criss-crossed by a complicated system of wires, with miniature cable cars, for the despatch of bills and receipts. C.D. sat at the central till, like a dark hairy spider in the middle of a web.

Evelyn's dress — a sensible green one — was duly bought, and we were shot out of the sprung door clutching our brown paper parcels. We had not got far when a hoarse voice summoned us from behind.

'Excuse me, Mrs Mawer.'

It was Eric Jenkins, Father's elderly photographic assistant, who suffered from chronic bronchitis. From years of incarceration in the developing room he also had difficulty in finding his way about. I watched him collapse on a public bench — the one erected outside the Nag's Head in memory of Alderman Wyn Davies. With an air of high drama he held out a note. This was in Father's usual telegraphic style of communication.

'Trip cancelled,' Mother read. 'Report to me without delay.'

With beating hearts we scurried through the Market Day crowds. Mother was convinced that Father must have had an accident. But this idea was contradicted by the sight of his bulky frame filling the entrance to the dispensary with vibrations of terrible energy.

His first utterance was mystifying.

'Sensible woman, Miss Davies,' he boomed. 'Never take chances with the French.'

All was made clear when he led us inside. Spread out on the dispensary counter, amidst the bottles and jars, was the afternoon edition of the *Liverpool Echo*. He rapped his spectacles on the largest headline. SUDETENLAND CRISIS, it ran, FRENCH ARMY VOW TO RESIST GERMAN INTER-VENTION. I had no idea where Sudetenland was but Father obviously knew.

'French Generals!' he snorted. 'They'll probably do no more than sit behind their Maginot Line. Even so, a crisis is a crisis, after all.'

'Well, Evelyn needed a summer dress anyway,' said Mother, always eager to look on the bright side of things.

'Well she'll have to do something to earn it,' Father said, 'and I have been doing a little thinking.'

We waited in trepidation to discover what awful plan had been coursing through his gingery head.

When he took out his black leather wallet I realised, with a sinking heart, that it concerned me. My school report was unfolded yet again, and Father's forefinger descended on the fatal line — FRENCH: 15 out of 100.

'There's going to be another kind of student exchange scheme,' he announced. 'Home based. At Resthaven.'

He took hold of my ear.

'This particular student is going to be exchanged for Something Better — a boy who gets 100 out of 100 for his French — after holiday tutorials by his eldest sister!'

The continental crisis subsided, but on the home front pressures escalated. My marks that autumn rose no higher than 50. However, this was deemed acceptable when Evelyn obtained her Distinction, particularly as for some strange reason there was a record crop of grapes that year. Seated at his iron-backed Leisure Chair in the conservatory, Father munched his way through another indigestible cluster.

'Only the French would think of fermenting fruit of this quality,' he said.

CHAPTER 16

CYNTHIA AND NEVILLE CHAMBERLAIN

'Your friend Cynthia will be having supper with us,' Father announced. We looked at one another in bemusement. Did we have a friend called Cynthia? My two elder sisters shook their heads and rolled their eyes heavenwards.

'She works in Father's dispensary,' my eldest sister Evelyn told me, as we were weeding the gravel by the front gate ready for Cynthia's visit.

'Father seems to think a lot of her.'

It was all very odd. Father never thought a lot of anybody.

'I wouldn't call her all that pretty,' added Constance Mary, spearing a large dandelion.

Cynthia turned out to be a mousy young lady with a tortoiseshell hair slide and a Claudette Colbert perm. Father's attitude to her was strictly patriarchal, touched with an elephantine roguishness which I found most disconcerting.

She was seated in the place of honour, on Father's right.

'How about a glass of ginger beer, Cynthia?' Father twinkled.

We all held our breath. Was she going to reply, 'Thank you, George'?

'Thank you, Mr Mawer,' she said demurely. We breathed again. The boundary line was clearly marked.

What else could she have called him? Nobody, apart from adult relatives, called him by his Christian name. And if she had referred to him as Uncle George, that, I am sure, would have spoiled things for Father.

Father's role fell into the Professor Higgins category — the Higgins of Shaw's play *Pygmalion*, I hasten to add, not the Rex Harrison version. He certainly saw her visits to Resthaven as being of a markedly improving nature. At the same time 'our friend' afforded him the novel sensation of flattery.

'Mr Mawer is so clever with pharmaceutical prescriptions,' she lisped. Like so many people who have an enunciation problem, she seemed inescapably drawn to words with a maximum of sibilants.

Mother nodded sweetly.

'Have another piece of bread and butter, Cynthia,' was all she said. Was there just a slight edge, I wondered, in her tone?

After the meal Cynthia ventured to ask if she could switch on the wireless to hear what Mr Chamberlain had to say about the world news.

'When you've helped clear the table,' Father directed from his chair, in no uncertain terms.

The rest of us registered silent approval. However singled out for favour at the dining table, Cynthia was still part of the workforce like everybody else.

With her domestic duties fulfilled, Father concentrated upon developing the powers of her mind. I remember he lent her an enormous volume entitled *Everything Within*. It had been acquired by him, free of charge, in return for a twelve-month subscription to the *News Chronicle*.

'Help to broaden her knowledge,' he explained to us later. 'In my view the girl has a great deal of potential.'

I was not sure of the exact nature of this mysterious attribute and did not dare to ask.

'Cynthia,' I was also informed, unlike me, was 'very quick on the uptake.'

Soon she was even partnering Father to victory at Kan U Go. Unfortunately the strain of trying to keep up to Father's exacting standards began to tell upon her.

'She looks as if she could do with some colour in her cheeks,' Father announced. He studied her wan features.

'We shall all go on an expedition to the Panorama Walk tomorrow, as it's Sunday.'

He glanced down at Cynthia's shoes — black patent leather with bows.

'You'll need something more substantial than those. Wellingtons, probably,' he said, as she made a dash through the downpour to catch the bus home.

The Panorama Walk, set in the hills beyond Wrexham, with its vistas of the Eglwyseg Rocks and the Dee Valley, was a favourite tourist attraction. Fortunately the day was fine and Father harnessed a camera around his neck, a Kodak Super-K on permanent loan from the shop.

In normal circumstances he took sole charge of its operation and every print had his unmistakable shadow falling across the scene. He always made sure that the sun was behind him and shining directly into the eyes of his victims.

This time he insisted on being in the photograph himself. To our surprise, my second sister was appointed to manipulate the Kodak. In her nervousness she clutched the camera to her chest with shaking hands. The resulting snap, developed in Mr Jenkin's dark room, had the Ruabon Mountain poised at a right angle as though a landslide was imminent. Even so, Father pasted the souvenir carefully into the family album. I still have it in my possession.

Down the tilted lane comes our exhausted procession, led by Father. He wears his dark grey weekend suit, wing collar, waistcoat, and boots. It is clearly a very hot day.

His hat — the grey trilby — makes him look rather like President Roosevelt at the presidential election campaign. He is gesticulating, with outstretched arm, to Cynthia by his side. She is obviously receiving a geological lecture of some kind.

The crouched figure in the middle ground is me, trying to tie up my shoe-lace for I think the twentieth time. Alongside are my sisters laden down with rugs and umbrellas.

I am not sure whether the blurred figure in the background, carrying a picnic basket, is Mother. She is shaded by a 1920s Leghorn straw hat, at least fifteen years out of date, which would be about right in Mother's case. But on further examination I'm inclined to guess that the figure with the basket is not Mother at all. It must be Edith, the maid. Probably Mother stayed at home, having 'a little bit of sewing' to do, and making the most of an unaccustomed peace.

The majority of Cynthia's visits were of course to Resthaven itself, and these would end with the inevitable reminder by her,

'Mr Mawer says I can take a jar of honey home with me.'

'Unless you're sweet enough already, Cynthia,' came Father's line, on cue. The rest of us gawked. Was there no end to Father's mood of bonhomie where our friend Cynthia was concerned?

The question we children constantly discussed amongst ourselves during that summer of 1939 was how long Father's indulgence towards Cynthia would last. There was, as yet, no sign of this unnatural state of affairs coming to an end. Indeed, they seemed to be getting even more chummy as the days went by.

'I think it would be a good idea,' Father suddenly announced, during the next session of Kan U Go, 'if

Cynthia took to The Wheel. It will serve her in good stead as she expands her career in the pharmaceutical industry.'

The hearse-like Austin Six (Father's last car before the Second World War began) was backed out of the garage. With a touch of malice Aunty Carrie pushed me out of the gate as gooseberry.

'The fresh air'll do him good too, Mr Mawer' she said. 'Cooped up with all them books all day and night.'

As usual, Aunty Carrie was barking up the wrong tree. Father's relationship with Cynthia was strictly platonic. I had only to sit in the back of the Austin and listen to the driving instruction to appreciate how far removed it was from even a hint of romance.

'Pay attention, Cynthia,' he would snap from the driving seat, as she sat tensely by his side, fiddling as usual with her Peter Pan collar.

'Notice how I change up gear by doubling the clutch,' the tutorial continued, 'with my left foot. Thus.' The car ricocheted forward.

'This petrol mix is too rich,' Father mumbled. 'Remind me to speak to Young Boot about it.'

He tried again.

'We'll drive as far as your parents' house,' he said, 'and then you can take over.'

Cynthia's father, Mr Edward Whale, was a market gardener. Every lesson began at the market garden. On each visit there we went through the same ritual. I would be engaged in tying on the L plates while Father was entertained to tea and cake by Cynthia and her mother. This was the opportunity for Mr Whale to load several unsolicited sackfuls of carrots into the back of the Austin. As Father emerged with his pupil, Mr Whale would spring forward and open the boot, revealing its bulging contents with the air of a conjuror.

'A good bit of nourishment for all the family,' he maintained, as Father took his place in the front passenger seat.

'That'll be half-a-crown,' he invariably added.

'Minus sixpence for the driving lesson,' was Father's quip in reply, as he produced a reluctant florin.

The lane outside was something of a corkscrew and Cynthia's progress was erratic. On the fourth lesson, she nearly ran down a pair of workmen painting white lines along the edge.

'That'll be a great help to learner drivers like me,' Cynthia said, sounding the horn a little too late.

Father straightened the wheel with a sigh.

'It'll be lights out for everybody if there's a war,' he said. 'I'm afraid Mr Chamberlain has to expect air-raid attacks. The white lines are to help people see in the dark.'

Cynthia giggled.

'Well Dad reckons his carrots do that. He says it's the Vitamin C.'

'I think your father had best leave the pharmaceutical aspects of his product to the professionals,' Father rejoined.

I could tell he was getting irritable. He turned to me.

'Stop bobbing about there, for heavens sake,' he exclaimed.

I was only trying to breathe some fresh air through the tiny grille in the roof to stave off the headache which usually preceded my dreaded car sickness.

There was no doubt that tensions were starting to build up on the driving lessons. Cynthia's mind began to be elsewhere. Mr Chamberlain was vying for her attention.

'He says if there's a war he'll need women in the Forces,' she said. Father snorted. That was the day he had designated for a test, the last Wednesday in August 1939, early closing at the shop and the beginning of a heat wave.

Father began as usual:

'Remember your sequence.

'Start the engine.

'Look in your driving mirror.

'Put the gear into first.

'Give your hand signal.

'Take off the brake.

'Let out the clutch.

'Accelerate gently.'

There was a hideous grinding sound from the gear box. Father turned red.

'How many times do I have to tell you not to mistake reverse for first gear,' he barked.

Cynthia was humming 'There'll Always Be An England' to herself, keeping up her spirits. The car stalled again.

'You've forgotten to take off the handbrake!' Father bellowed.

His neck was now purple.

'Engine!

'Gear!

'Signal!

'Brake!

'Clutch!

'Hand signal!'

Father had lost control. Or rather he had reverted to his normal style of communication, in other words, a series of explosions.

'A very poor effort,' he pronounced. 'Hopeless. Totally hopeless!'

All of a sudden it was too much for Cynthia. The humming stopped. She let go of the wheel and burst into tears. The car ran gently into a field.

I remained on the rear floor where the roughness of the ground had thrown me. I could hear Father breathing heavily in between Cynthia's blubs. Through the gap between the front seats I saw him bring out a handker-

chief. Cynthia ignored it, struggled out of the car, and
flounced away through the long grass.

Along the lane appeared the Marchwiel bus. I sat up
and watched her step aboard. Cynthia and the bus disappeared in a cloud of dust.

Father moved into the driving seat and drove home in
complete silence.

A huge rift had obviously been opened. My sisters kept
me informed of developments. For three days Cynthia
did not turn up for work at the shop. I was told that she
had complained to her parents that Mr Knox Mawer had
bullied her and that she was even thinking of giving in
her notice.

'I've given that girl an ultimatum,' Father announced
at Friday lunch-time.

'If she doesn't report for duty this weekend, that's an
end of it.'

We were all agog. What was going to happen? The
message had been delivered to Cynthia's home by Mr
Jenkins who, on the rare occasions that he was not in the
developing room, apparently lived at Marchwiel, not far
from the market garden.

By a strange coincidence a parallel crisis was looming
on the international front. According to the headlines in
Father's *Daily Mail*, the German Army was massed on
the Polish frontier. The British Ambassador in Berlin had
delivered a final communiqué. Mr Chamberlain was waiting to hear from Herr Hitler.

On the Sunday morning Father's ultimatum ran out. So
did Mr Chamberlain's.

'I have to tell you now,' announced the Prime Minister,
as we gathered around the wireless set, 'this country is
at war with Germany.'

Father nodded.

'A question of misplaced trust.' he announced.

We all caught his meaning.

There were no more visits to Resthaven by Cynthia. We heard that she had joined the ATS at Chester, where she was advanced to the post of Driver/Corporal. Father was not informed. Her name was never mentioned in the family again.

CHAPTER 17

FAMILY ROOTS

Mile after mile of brussels-sprouts, row upon row of tur-
nips, a thousand cabbages stretching glumly into the
bleak horizon of Freiston Fen — I was not surprised that
this was Father's birthplace.

Even so, for what turned out to be our last family
excursion in peace time, it seemed a strange choice of
venue. According to Father, however, the Mawers were
still at large in that neighbourhood.

'I have to see your Great-Aunt Lilian,' he said, by way
of explanation.

To make the considerable journey from Wrexham, he
had hired another car from Young Boot (now approaching
his sixty-third birthday). 'The new Morris Ten with big
sit-back-and-enjoy-yourself-seats-on-runners' was how it
was described in the brochure flourished by Young Boot.

Sitting back and enjoying himself was naturally not
Father's way, although he did go so far as to concede
that on this occasion he would 'combine business with
pleasure'.

The first of these pleasures was the icy plunge, next
morning, into the North Sea, for which we were all con-
scripted, apart from Mother. Fortunately it was only a
short walk back to our rented chalet on the mud flats at
Freiston, where Mother had hot drinks awaiting us.

'What's your opinion, Clara?' Father asked suddenly.
Mother paused in surprise, his second spoonful of Horlicks still unmixed. Her opinion on things was rarely
sought.

'Could this boy be trusted to collect the papers from Jebb and Tunnard?'

'Of course he could,' Mother insisted.

Jebb and Tunnard turned out to be the Mawer family solicitors, in Wide Bargate, Boston. Father continued his instructions for me with an even more mysterious rider.

'Then he has to bring the documents along to me at Inglenook One.'

Clearing his throat, Father proceeded to volunteer a few more details. It emerged that Great-Aunt Lilian and her husband Captain Charles Mawer had had a bizarre domestic relationship. For forty-six years they had chosen to reside in adjourning semi-detached villas, in Freiston Road, Boston — Inglenook One (Alderman Lilian Mawer) and Inglenook Two (the Captain). Not surprisingly, in view of this arrangement, they had no children.

Arriving in Freiston Road, after two long bus rides, I noticed that the curtains of Inglenook Two were still drawn, even though the Captain had died four weeks earlier. Perhaps, I thought, the Alderman was more attached to Great-Uncle Charles than otherwise believed.

I was standing at the gate of Inglenook One when Father's Morris drew up with a peremptory toot. I immediately handed him the large buff envelope obtained from Jebb and Tunnard. Holding it in front of him like a breast plate, Father walked up to the front door and knocked loudly. For some minutes there was no reply. Then a shrill female voice rang out from above his trilby-covered head.

'Who's there?'

Father stepped back. The voice came from a small wooden balcony built out over the front porch. The area was a mass of foliage, grown from potted plants of all varieties.

'Is that you, Aunt Lilian?' Father called up.

The lady herself was invisible.

'It's Alderman Lilian Mawer,' replied a voice from the balcony jungle.

'Who are you?'

'I'm your nephew, George Knox Mawer,' Father explained.

'And who's that scraggy-looking boy by the gate?'

'I'm afraid that's my son.'

'What do you want?' Father was asked.

'To talk about the disposal of Uncle Charles's estate,' he replied.

'Well you can both clear off immediately,' declared Great-Aunt Lilian, who had still not revealed herself.

'But I've come all the way from Wrexham,' Father began.

I could hardly believe the apologetic note in his voice. I had never seen him encounter someone even more formidable than himself.

'I don't care if you've come all the way from Timbuctoo,' the voice rasped. Inquisitive curtains twitched at the side window of the next house down the road.

'I was married to a Mawer for forty-seven years, and I never want to see another one as long as I live!'

'Blood is surely thicker than water, Aunt Lil,' Father faltered, flapping the envelope.

No doubt he thought he was entitled to a legacy. If not for himself, then for me, his only male offspring. He was to be rudely disappointed upon both counts.

'Are you going away or not?' snapped Alderman Mawer.

'I'd still like to pay my respects,' Father insisted, standing his ground. Great-Aunt Lilian must have been watering her plants. The next moment a steady stream descended over Father's trilby.

'Well you can have that with *my* respects,' was the final rejoinder from the chatelaine of Inglenook One.

With some dignity Father shook out the hat, before

retracing his steps to the Morris. I brought up the rear, trying not to run. He leaned across to close the front door upon my side.

'Of course she's only a Mawer by marriage,' he said, 'if you could call it that.'

He started up the car engine.

'Can't understand how your Great-Uncle Charles stayed the course for all those years,' he continued, driving slowly into Boston Square. 'As far as I know, she never cooked him a single meal.'

Father parked by the church, took out his reading spectacles, and began to study the contents of the Jebb and Tunnard envelope. Emboldened by fellow sympathy I dared to ask, 'Any luck Father?' His gaze concentrated on the final line of an impressive legal document.

'To George Robert Knox and his son,' Father read out, 'my shares in the Boston Gas Company *at the discretion of my widow*.'

There was a silence, broken at last by a loud ripping sound. Father had torn the parchment into half, and half again.

'Go and put that in the nearest rubbish unit,' was all he said.

On my return, Father brought out his gold hunter watch.

'The question now,' he continued, 'is how the three hours I had set aside for the abortive visit to Inglenook One can be put to another purpose.'

He consulted his Rotarians' pocket diary.

'A lucky thing it's a Tuesday,' he said, 'I shall be in good time for the weekly luncheon of the Boston Rotary Club at the Peacock Hotel.'

He handed me a shilling.

'Go over to Cotton's Grocery Store and buy yourself a pork pie and a bottle of milk.'

When I returned with the purchases Father was straightening his wing collar and tie in the driving mirror.

'Things have worked out very conveniently,' he declared, 'in spite of that wretched woman.' He opened the glove compartment. It seemed that I was to be usefully employed as well.

'There's some reading here for you to get on with while I'm away.'

He drew out a musty tome of enormous weight, bound in cloth. I opened the flyleaf. *The History and Antiquities of Boston, With The Village Of Swineshead, Freiston, and Slippery-Goute, By The Reverend J Fitzwilliam Butler MA* it read.

'One family possession that Aunt Lilian hasn't got her hands on,' Father observed. 'Belonged to your great-grandfather.'

Since the pages of the Reverend Butler's life work were entirely uncut, it was plain that neither Great-Grandfather nor Father had ever consulted it.

'Use these,' he said, handing me the pharmaceutical scissors from his waistcoat pocket, 'with care,'

Father heaved himself out of the driving seat. It had started to rain.

'No doubt I shall be hearing a few uncomplimentary things concerning Alderman Lilian Mawer's background, from one or other of the Boston Rotarians,' he observed, as he put up his umbrella and stalked away.

By the time Father returned, shortly after three p.m., I had sliced my way through all the dusty chapters of Great-Grandad's tome.

'Just as I would have guessed,' Father reported, hic-coughing loudly. The post-prandial digestive process had begun. 'Two of Lilian Mawer's fellow members of council were at the luncheon. The woman comes from Absolutely Nothing. Pure sour grapes on her part, over the Mawer

family tree. An inferiority complex from the very beginning where Uncle Charles was concerned.'

I had discovered five entries in the *History of Boston*
relating to the Mawers. The first four were all too easily
memorised.

'1493, Peter Mawer, fenn-slodger, convicted of coining
at Lincoln Assize. Subsequently hanged.'

'1589, Simon Mawer, committed suicide. Buried at
Crossroads, Skirbeck, in unhallowed ground.'

'1647, Alfred Mawer, branded at Toadbridge for petty
larceny.'

'1708, Mathew Mawer, killed in an affray at
Swineshead.'

'Did you read up about the family,' Father enquired,
when we set off back to the beach chalet. I did a rapid bit
of mental censorship.

'Oh yes, Father,' I replied turning up entry number
five. 'It says here that John Mawer enrolled with the
Honourable East India Company Marine in 1787.'

'Yes indeed,' Father enthused, 'the beginning of a most
distinguished career. Typical of every generation of the
family.'

He glanced sharply in my direction.

'Let us hope I have not produced the first one to let the
side down.'

CHAPTER 18

FATHER AND THE WAR EFFORT

The lead-up to the war was heralded at Resthaven by a strange postal delivery, the most memorable of Father's Bulk Orders. He had been studying the columns of *The Chemist and Druggist*.

'It will be totally against the national interest, Clara,' he remarked, 'for my sleep to be disturbed by air-raids. We pharmacists will need to be on the qt from dawn to dusk for the supply of emergency medications.'

A few weeks later Mr Boyo Evans, the post office van driver, staggered up our front drive with an enormous cardboard box. From my weeding station on the herbaceous border I darted forward to take a look. The huge container was stamped all over with what looked like instructions in German.

'It's for your father,' said the postman, 'maybe Mr Hitler has sent him a birthday present!'

At that moment the side door opened.

'If you don't need the stamps, Mr Mawer,' said Boyo, depositing the parcel at Father's feet, 'my sister would like them.' He was as keen as I was to penetrate the mystery. 'She hasn't got any German ones.'

'The consignment is from Sweden,' Father said coldly, 'so not surprisingly the stamps are Swedish.'

He closed the door behind him. Meanwhile I had nipped inside through the French window.

From behind the grandfather clock I watched Father bring out his surgical scissors. He extracted two curious white objects from one of the packets, which he inserted into his ears. Looking rather like Bugs Bunny, he took as many boxes as he could carry up to the bathroom. I seized the chance to inspect the lettering on the container. EAR STOPPLES, it read, 144 BOXEN GROSSE. KRONOR 152.

I quickly passed on the news to the rest of the family. 'They're the latest in ear-plugs,' Mother explained, 'for blocking out all external noise.'

Perhaps, I thought, life would now take a happier turn. With Father bunged up in his bedroom from 9.30 each night, I would be free to tune in to Stainless Stephen, my favourite comic on the wireless. But alas, this was not to be.

Father arrived home for lunch on the first Monday of Hostilities with the *Amended Radio Times* under his arm.

'Well at least the BBC is setting a good example, Clara,' he commented.

As soon as he had left for the shop, I turned over the pages, planning more secret listening — the Western Brothers, 'a couple of cads', and Arthur Askey with Stinker Murdoch in 'Band Wagon'. To my dismay the BBC had scrapped everything. Under a bleak grey photograph of Broadcasting House I was offered nothing more than the national news at hourly intervals, with 'Gramophone Records' in between, of a most dismal variety. No longer, it seemed, was I to hear from the Accordion Ragamuffins. The nearest thing to light music would be Gracie Fields soaring into 'Land of Hope and Glory'.

Father wholly approved of this 'expecting the worst' approach. He was extremely irritated, therefore, when after a short period the 'phoney war' developed and normal programmes returned — except that dance bands now played under the banner of The Forces Programme.

The Forces Sweetheart was Miss Vera Lynn, whose message was 'Keep Smiling Through'. Judging from the expression on Father's face, that was the last thing he intended to do. Much more to his way of thinking were the grim government posters stuck up on the walls of the Town Hall, all in funereal black lettering.

GO TO IT.
DON'T WASTE FOOD.
CARELESS TALK COSTS LIVES.
DIG FOR VICTORY.
USE SHANKS PONY.

I studied the slogans with a shock of recognition. They had a chilling familiarity, as though Father himself had composed them. What else had we ever done at Resthaven except GO TO IT?. From the moment when dawn broke over the cracked slates outside my bedroom window until the candle was snuffed out in Edith's adjoining closet, we had all of us been doing precisely that.

Nor had any of us ever dared to WASTE FOOD. No dinner plate of mine was permitted to leave the dining-room table unless scraped meticulously clean. 'Does that boy think I'm blind, Clara? I can see perfectly well that he's left a piece of crackling under his fork.'

And as for CARELESS TALK, that had been something to be indulged only in whispered undertones behind the tightly closed kitchen door. My imitation of Father rehearsing his Masonic ritual in the bathroom always had Aunty Carrie in stitches. But my performance was given at grave risk to limb, if not life, because Father had the sinister knack of entering Resthaven through the side door in deadly silence. His high-pitched bark, 'What's going on in here?' was the first indication given of his presence. The green baize curtains parted and there he would be, like the genie in a pantomime.

Then there was the injunction DIG FOR VICTORY. That was something I had been doing long before the outbreak of hostilities — digging for Father's victory, at least. At the time of Munich, 1938, he had bought me a pair of studded farming boots, having an excessive fondness for new potatoes.

'Bound to be a shortage of Cheshires, Clara,' he explained, 'when the balloon goes up. I've bought some tubers for him to trench in.' Mother inspected the all-weather double soles, with iron toe-caps and half-metal heels.

'They're awfully heavy, George.'

'The heavier the better.'

The DIG FOR VICTORY poster showed a blade being thrust into the soil by the instep of an enormous black boot. It looked remarkably like mine.

The poster USE SHANKS PONY was equally familiar. That expression had been on Father's lips for as long as I could remember. When I first heard the mysterious injunction I pictured an actual pony being produced for me, since George Owen came to school from his father's farm in a horse and trap.

'There's certainly no need for him to waste a penny on a bus ride, Clara, when he can use Shanks Pony.'

My school was three miles away from Resthaven. On wet days Mother would peer out anxiously.

'It's awfully wet, George.'

'A bit of rain won't harm him. There isn't a bus for half an hour anyway, and I'm not having him here, lounging about the house.'

Now that the nation was at war, Lounging About The House became a form of treachery in Father's view. Not that there was a chair at Resthaven in which one could even try to lounge. What Father had in mind was nothing less than frenzied hyperactivity.

To ensure that during the national emergency we were kept in this condition Father had delivered by Dodd's delivery van a large number of hessian strips.

'What exactly are they for, George?' Mother enquired.

'Rug-making,' she was told.

He drew from his wallet an explanatory cutting from the *Daily Mail*. 'We have to make our own luxuries from now on. Relieve the pressure on the Merchant Navy.'

Resthaven had never been over-full of luxuries.

'How are the rugs made, dear?'

He pointed to a large sack delivered with the hessian strips.

'With droppings,' he said.

I peered inside, expecting the worst. In fact this was a term used for the remnants from the wool factory, all of a uniform mud colour.

While we remained in the house and embarked upon rug-making, Father was busy organising the shopkeepers of High Street into a firefighting team. He would return home to glare at my lack of progress with fierce displeasure.

'He's all fingers and thumbs, Clara,' he complained.

What I had to do was thread the pieces of wool into the hessian strips with a huge bobbin. It was rather like sewing mail bags, but no prisoner at Walton Jail had a more vigorous supervisor.

'What do we do with them when they're finished, George?' Mother asked.

'They're for insulation,' Father answered. He jabbed his finger on the *Daily Mail* cutting.

'Help in the battle for fuel,' it said, 'by keeping doors padded against draughts'.

My unevenly surfaced handiwork was tried out by the front door, providing a danger trap for Mrs Jarvis Roberts when she strode briskly across our threshold, next day. She was in her bottle green WVS uniform with a matching brimmed hat and gleaming badge.

'I've come to enlist Ronnie's aid in our national savings campaign,' she said.

'As soon as he's got the lumps out of that rug,' Father agreed.

About half an hour later I was allowed to put on my school cap and follow her out through the gate. It was a hot day. I was reminded of my favourite song from last night's programme of Henry Hall and the BBC Dance Orchestra.

'Just direct your feet to the sunny side of the street,' the Fol-de-rols had warbled.

I started to hum the melody as I distributed Mrs Jarvis Roberts's leaflets to the houses with even numbers.

'Leave your troubles on the doorstep,' had been Henry Hall's message. The problem was that when I got home again my trouble was waiting on the doorstep, precisely where I had left it.

'Five minutes late,' Father complained, 'I distinctly told Mrs Jarvis Roberts to have you here by five-fifteen. You've missed most of the programme already.'

The wireless was turned up to its maximum volume.

'Her Royal Highness the Princess Elizabeth is addressing the children of the Empire on the contribution to the War Effort,' he said. Constance Mary and Rosemary were sitting respectfully on either side of the Marconi speaker.

'My sister the Princess Margaret and I,' said a squeaky voice, 'are thinking about you all, and the hardships we face together in our homes.' I pictured Buckingham Palace strewn with mud-coloured hessian strips to keep out the draught.

A few months later, the rugs completed, Father's attention was caught by a Ministry of Information directive. A large leaflet fluttered through the letter-box. Father brought it into us. 'HOUSEHOLDERS! ADOPT A SERVICEMAN', it was headed.

'The least we can do,' Father read aloud, 'is to provide a pleasant little parlour evening for the lonely soldier or airman at the nearest camp.'

There was a long silence.

'Did you hear me?' Father demanded.

Mother and I looked up from our current 'war efforts'. I was counting milk-bottle tops — SILVER PAPER MEANS A SILVER LINING — while Mother was hard at work with her Singer sewing machine, the personification of MRS SEW AND SEW of the Government slogan urging us to MAKE DO AND MEND, something Mother was well used to.

'Can't think why I didn't think of it before, Clara,' Father said, having gained our attention. He placed the leaflet on the table between us, and pointed to the picture on the back, showing just such a social evening. The genial host wore a welcoming beam, a cardigan and carpet slippers. A tray of hot drinks steamed in the background while he slipped a record onto a radiogram for the amusement of two young men in airforce uniform seated in a laughing family circle. Mother and I had the same silent thought.

Nobody could have less resembled the host in the photograph than Father. Nor did we own a radiogram.

'We may not have one of those record machines, Clara, 'Father continued, 'but R.J. Evans, the harmonium player at the lodge, might manage a tuning job on the upright piano.'

He glanced severely in my direction.

'Unless that boy had ruined it beyond repair with his so-called piano lessons.'

I shook my head reassuringly.

'Perhaps we could even have what they call a sing-song with some of the boys from the barracks.'

I pictured the rolling drunks, who frequently passed the house on their way back to camp after closing time, being received by Mother and Aunty Carrie.

'I'm sure Ronnie will manage a bit of playing,' Mother said, 'but we'll need some music.' She glanced hastily at the only scores on the stand, *Hymns Ancient and Modern* and Schubert's *Song without Words*.

Next day Father despatched me to Crane's music shop in Regent Street.

'Get a modern piece by this BBC chap Henry Hall,' he directed. He handed me twopence. This restricted me to the less popular hits. I came back with something called 'Toodle-oo'. At least the words of the chorus did not strike me as overdemanding, from a soldier's point of view.

> Toodle-oo til tomorrow, sweet dreams to you,
> Nighty night, sleep tight, toodle-oo.
> Toodle-oo, soon the sandman will call on you
> Nighty night, sleep tight, toodle-loo.

Back at Resthaven Father had instructed Edith to light a fire in the drawing-room.

'Are they coming already?' I asked.

'I have sent Mr Jenkins with a note to the Adjutant,' Father replied, 'so we should be prepared.'

The rest of the family were summoned. With Father towering menacingly over my shoulder, I was required to play the melody.

Then to our intense surprise and embarrassment, Father began to sing the words.

'Don't rattle through it,' he instructed sternly, 'an even tempo is what's required.'

What Father's voice lacked in musicality — he was entirely tuneless — he more than made up for in force and determination.

'Toodle-oo til tomorrow, sweet dreams to you,' he enunciated solemnly. 'Nighty-night, sleep tight, toodle-loo.'

I paused, overwhelmed by the incongruity of the exercise.

'Carry on. Carry on,' Father reprimanded. I carried on.

'Toodle-oo,' Father continued with even greater emphasis, 'soon the sandman will call on you.' Every word was pronounced with great clarity.

There was an interval, during which we were delegated to 'go and cut some sandwiches'. A tin of corned beef was brought up from the cellar for this purpose.

By the time two hours had gone by, it became evident that our guests had decided to fight shy. Bedtime arrived. As we trekked upstairs, Father could be heard winding the clock. Nothing if not thorough, he was still practising his sing-song.

'Toodle-oo til tomorrow, sweet dreams to you,'

In Father's interpretation, the words sounded like a command.

'Nighty-night, sleep tight, toodle-loo.'

CHAPTER 19

A TRAITOR IN THE RANKS

In the summer of 1940, Britain and Father stood at bay.
In the words of Winston Churchill, 'the entire population
labours to the last limit of its strength . . . the beaches
bristle with defences . . . the factories pour out
weapons . . . the army drills from morn til night . . .
when rifles are lacking the Home Guard grasps lustily the
shot-gun, the sporting rifle, the pistol, the pike, and the
club.' As far as I could see, all Father would have to hand
would be his celebrated apothecary's pestle. This was a
large blunt instrument made of granite, handed down by
his predecessor and kept in the glass cabinet which
shielded the Jeyes toilet refills from public view. This
would certainly come in useful, I reflected, if German
parachutists arrived. With the possibility of armed conflict
in Wrexham's High Street, Father had turned the back
premises of the pharmacy into an Emergency Dressing
Station. Its general appearance — with a forest of crutches
and splints in one corner and a small mountain of red
flannel blankets in the other — reminded me of an illus-
tration from the Crimean War in my history book.

Perhaps, I fantasised, Father would confuse the foe by
camouflaging himself with his bee-keeper's veil. I was
sure that whatever happened he would face his end at
the hands of the Gestapo in the full Masonic dress of the
North Wales Grand Arch Chapter.

During my long school holiday, while the Battle of Britain was fought out in the sky, Father ensured that I
played my part on the ground. He arranged for me to

work on the farm of his colleague, Worshipful Brother Ernest Hopkin of Plas Eglwyseg, Ruabon. This involved a journey of seven miles each way. At first Father maintained that this was no more than a brisk walk there and back. When Brother Hopkin pointed out that it would only leave me four hours of actual work, Father agreed that some other form of transport would be needed.

'Come and see what he's got for you,' Mother said eagerly that evening, after family cocoa. She led me into the back yard. My spirits rose. Then fell again. Propped up against the wash-house door was the errand boy's bike from the shop. The boy, a middle-aged man called Eric, had enlisted in the navy.

Upon the huge iron basket attached to the handlebars was painted Father's familiar slogan, FEELING ILL IN WREXHAM? VISIT THE PHARMACY AT 9 HIGH STREET. DELIVERY SERVICE FREE.

'He should manage a good turn of speed,' Father declared over breakfast next day, in the early light of dawn. 'Especially on those country lanes.'

Just to make sure, he made a point of telephoning Worshipful Brother Hopkin, to check upon my time of arrival.

'Your father says have you got here yet?' was my daily greeting for the next four weeks.

Double summer-time had been introduced, a scheme heartily endorsed by Father since it added another hour to my labours in the cornfield. Night was falling when I trundled back to Resthaven with the aid of a carbide lamp. Every attempt to take a nap during the daytime had been rewarded by a sharp prod from Mr Hopkin's harvest pikle and the words 'You wouldn't want your father to know about this, would you?'

As a result I found myself nodding off over the wheel. On one occasion I woke up to find myself catapulted into one of the trenches dug on the roadside for troop defence against the impending invasion. However, I consoled myself with the knowledge that father's labour camp regime served to take my mind off the thought of my School Certificate Examination results. These were expected any day now.

I invariably reached home in time to report for the nine o'clock news. This was a solemn moment in every household when families gathered around the wireless set to hear Alvar Liddell read the latest bulletin on the progress of the war. On September 15th there was a special announcement: the Prime Minister was to speak to the nation. It was the famous occasion when Mr Churchill paid tribute to the victory of the Royal Air Force in the air.

'Never in the field of human conflict,' he announced in ringing tones, 'was so much owed by so many to so few.'

Fixing me with a baleful glare, Father zoomed in on cue.

'Never in the field of human endeavour was so little achieved for so long by one slothful boy,' he declaimed. Solemnly he held up his copy of the *Evening Leader* folded back at the middle. The section was filled with the long columns of the Central Welsh Board School Certificate results. Down towards the bottom of the page, I glimpsed with a sinking heart, my own name, encircled in magenta ink. A threatening silence intervened.

Mr Churchill was winding up his peroration. 'This,' he declared, 'was their finest hour.' It certainly wasn't mine.

As usual Mother tried to intervene on my behalf.

'Still, he has managed a pass, George,' she said quietly.

'Scraped is the word, Clara,' Father corrected.

Mother tried again. 'He did quite well in scripture, dear. And he got a credit in Music.'

Father chose to ignore these irrelevancies and sat down to his cold collation – spam and under-ripe tomatoes from the greenhouse.

'I've been making some detailed calculations,' he continued. 'There are a hundred and fifty names in this list. In order of merit your Son has succeeded in achieving the outstanding position of 145th.' He sliced explosively into a large green tomato. The removal of several pips from the front of his steel-rimmed glasses occupied the next few moments.

Flinging down his napkin again, he returned to the attack.

'And that's counting his passes in English Language and English Literature as two subjects. Which they most certainly are not.'

'But George,' Mother continued.

'But nothing,' came the reply. 'According to the *Daily Mail* the Prime Minister reckons we've no Fifth Column in this country. I'm afraid that is untrue. We have a traitor at this very table. A traitor to the family.'

He pointed a quivering finger in the direction of the hallway.

'Why do you think I have had the exemplary Matriculation Certificates of his sisters framed and hung where he cannot fail to see them as he walks past every day — even with that appalling stoop of his?'

There was another silence. As always, Father quickly supplied his own answer to his question.

'It was in the hope that the boy would keep up the family record of academic distinction! That record has now been blotched forever.' As a punctuation mark, a loud hiccough followed. The bottle of Stone ginger beer at his elbow had been drained more rapidly than ever.

The dinnerplates were removed by Mother and Edith on tiptoe. Father ladled out the fruit and custard, allowing me just one small plum. Just as I was steeling myself for a further analysis of my scholastic shortcomings, Field Marshall Göring came to my rescue. The Commander-in-Chief of the German air force had decreed that this was the moment to launch his raid on Merseyside. Even Father could not compete with the high-pitched whine of the air-raid siren.

'All down to the shelter,' he ordered. He had converted the first of the four cellars under Resthaven and now led the way down the steps, impervious to the smell of rotting potatoes and our faulty gas main. No one else I knew had arranged a ready-made underground bunker. 'Thinking ahead' had once again put him one up on the rest of the local population, particularly our neighbours the Herford Jenkins. Major Herford Jenkins, with his military expertise, had rashly claimed that the German Air Force would confine itself to the south of England.

'Perhaps we ought to ask them to join us,' Mother suggested. 'There's plenty of room for them, especially as the girls are away.'

Father's reply consisted of one of his Delphic pronouncements.

'He who makes his bed must lie in it!'

Father's bed, in this instance, comprised a strange folding contraption he had set up in the corner. Here he rapidly installed himself after removing his jacket. Over his shirt he majestically donned an elephantine pair of pyjamas, second best, blue striped. His 'bunker outfit' was completed by a grey flannel bed jacket, one of a dozen ordered in bulk from the Army Surplus Stores in Queen Street.

Equipped with eiderdowns, Mother, Edith and I managed to make ourselves comfortable upon trestle tables erected on the other side of the room. Outside I could here the distant thud of anti-aircraft guns and the drone of enemy planes.

'We must all try to get some sleep,' Mother whispered.

In his corner Father was very much awake. By the light of a Tilly lamp from the garden shed he was irascibly turning over the remaining pages of the *Wrexham Leader*.

'Hello. What's this?' he suddenly called out.

On the verge of sleep I shot up with a violent start.

'Anything wrong, dear?' Mother ventured from the gloomy shadows on our side of the cellar.

Father was peering hard at something that had caught his eye on the back page, where the advertisements appeared.

'School Leaver required,' he read out. 'For St Giles Parish Church. To replace regular organ blower, now on active service. No qualifications necessary. Some appreciation of sacred music and biblical knowledge an advantage.' He paused. 'Now that would be one possible opening for the boy, at least, Clara,' he said.

In the gloom I could not see whether he was speaking seriously or not.

'Perhaps I should have a word with the vicar tomorrow morning!'

As he spoke the wail of the siren told us that the air-raid was over.

'All clear,' Father pronounced.

On the contrary, I thought, as I trudged despairingly up to bed. Never had my own particular situation seemed more confused or confusing.

CHAPTER 20

THE COMFORTS OF HOME

Father did not go in for letters. I had joined up and news from Resthaven came in war-standard envelopes addressed to 14438573 Private Mawer, R K, wherever he happened to be. They were always penned by Mother. That is to say, they were in her small round hand on pale blue note paper. But the presence of a ghost writer was manifest in practically every other sentence. Had I still not tried for a commission? . . . Did I know that Donald Rathwell was already a captain? . . . Was I aware of the dire influence of the notorious drinking habits and foul language in the ranks . . . Surely I was not making proper use of the expensive education given to me . . .

I might be doing my modest best for King and country in the national hour of need, yet as far as Father was concerned I was still in school uniform. To make matters worse, I was now faced with the dismal prospect of two weeks home leave before my regiment sailed for India. However, I arrived at Resthaven to encounter an uncanny peace: Father was in hospital.

'Nothing serious,' Mother assured me, as we set off to visit him with a bunch of his favourite sour grapes from the stunted vine in the conservatory.

'There are two tickets in my dressing-gown pocket, Clara,' the patient said, when Mother and I were seated on the end of his bed.

'What tickets are those, George?'

'I've arranged for this boy to take Alison Gould to the Masonic Ball.'

Father had often referred to his colleague Worshipful Brother Doctor Dickson Gould, the North Wales Provincial Arch Mason, although I had never met his daughter Alison. I was about to voice some sort of protest about having my private life organised in this cavalier way, when Mother intervened.

'There's no need to worry about that now, dear,' she told him, 'wait until we've got you safely home.'

She took hold of my arm.

'Don't upset him,' she whispered, 'not so soon after his operation.'

The operation had been to remove all his teeth. Apparently his 'wisdoms' had been condemned and Father was not given to half measures. Judging by the trouble he was causing to the nursing staff — from matron down, he was already back to normal health. He arrived home only two days later with a chillingly false smile provided by his new teeth.

'One thing the Army should have taught him, Clara,' he said, adjusting the gaunt angle of his arm-chair, 'is an appreciation of the Comforts of Home.'

His references to me continued in the third person as though I were a mere phantom whose true self was still far away in P Battery of The Royal Horse Artillery.

'I'm sure Ronnie's very happy to be back in his old room for a while, dear,' Mother agreed.

I was anxious not to appear ungrateful, although 'Ronnie's room' was now rather on the small side. After all, I had been away for nearly two years, and seemed to be still growing. There was also the familiar problem of the water cistern. This was boxed into a large wooden sarcophagus occupying half the bedroom space, with a labyrinth of ancillary pipes precariously clustered above my pillow. It kept me awake in the night with excruciating groans and gurgles. Not that there was much danger of sleep. The icy draught through the ill-fitting casement was worse than any gun emplacement. And each time the eiderdown caught between the bedstead and the rickety bookcase alongside, down came my *Boys' Own Annual 1927–34* and Arthur Mee's *Childrens' Encyclopaedia*, Abattoir to Zulu. I switched on the reading lamp, pulled my army great-coat around me, and embarked upon the Zulu Wars.

There was a sharp rapping on the wall at the foot of the stairs leading up to the third storey.

'His light's still on Clara.'

Did he expect me to read in the dark? I thought mutinously.

However, when I came down for breakfast next morning I found Father in a friendlier mood. Indeed, his flashing dentures seemed to impose an uncharacteristic bonhomie upon him. At least for a short while.

'He can have the use of the errand boy's cycle,' he announced unexpectedly, as he portioned out our wartime rations of bacon. Nor did he raise any objections to my using this antedeluvian machine — with its iron basket affixed to the front handlebars — for visiting the Majestic Cinema, the former roller-skating rink, for the second house of *The Fleet's In*, starring Betty Hutton. Father was under the impression that this was an educational film recording British Naval History.

'Remember,' he warned, 'the doors at Resthaven are locked at 9 p.m.'

It was Aunty Carrie who found me a key to the side door. Just as well, because Betty Hutton's exploits ran half an hour overtime, with the usual breakdown in the Majestic's projection room. The Wrexham Parish Church clock was striking ten when I arrived back home. To my surprise there was still a chink of light through the blackout curtain in the wireless room. Father had obviously stayed up to listen to J. B. Priestley's 'Postscript'.

'A bit better than that dreadful American, Raymond

Gramm Swing. Not that you'd expect much from a man with a name like that.'

I decided that if I could get safely indoors, I would pretend to come down the stairs as though I had been back in my room since curfew time. I'd reckoned without the gravel, which Father had had layered in enormously thick drifts on the main path. 'Best to buy in bulk' remained his maxim, despite wartime shortages. There was a ghastly crunching sound from the wheels of the errand boy's cycle as I pushed it furtively past the window. The only solution was to pick it up and carry it. How was I to know that Father's wheelbarrow had been positioned at the bottom of the steps leading up to the french window? Nor could I have expected it to be full of empty tin cans — corned beef and baked beans, Father's favourite food at the time. I remembered, then, the MOI Poster which he had pinned up on the greenhouse door — TURN RAW MATERIAL INTO WAR MATERIAL.

'What the devil!' I heard Father explode.

There was the sound of the French window being furiously unbarred.

As he emerged I was still having trouble with the bicycle chain, which was locked in the jaws of one of the corned beef tins. I was trying to focus the beam of the cycle lamp on the problem.

'Is he deliberately trying to attract the attention of a German bomber, Clara?'

In point of fact, silhouetted against the lighted entrance, Father himself was a far more attractive target for a passing Heinkel.

'Put that light out,' called Mr Elwyn Jones, the Grosvenor Road ARP warden. The nearest Wrexham had got to an enemy bomber was a stray Barrage Balloon which had broken free from its moorings above the gasworks, but Mr Elwyn Jones was ever watchful.

'My fault, Mr Jones,' I shouted back, 'just arrived on embarkation leave.'

'Quick thinking,' Father said, considerably mollified by my saving him from a possible fine. 'Officious little so-and-so.'

Father was still in a good humour the following morning. With a flourish he produced the dreaded tickets for the Masonic Ball which I had hoped were forgotten.

'He can borrow my old dinner jacket, Clara,' he said expansively. 'I'll be wearing my new one.'

This was the first doom-laden indication I had received that he himself was planning to attend as well.

For the next hour he looked in and out of the sewing room, keeping an eye on the necessary operations. Mother was required laboriously to move the buttons on the old dinner jacket and re-press the lapel so as to transform it from single to double breasted style. Even so, it was still hopelessly large for me, and not surprisingly Alison found my appearance an ill-concealed disappointment.

'I suppose there's not much call in the ranks for black tie occasions,' she observed. It was too much of a black tie occasion for me, sitting stiffly at the wheel of her father's gleaming Ford V8 in my shapeless attire.

'At least I thought the Army would have taught you how to drive,' she added, as I maimed the large gnome fishing in her father's lily pond. There was an angry knocking from the mullioned lounge window, but I decided it was best not to stop. Dr Gould had offered me his car upon being informed that my only form of transport was the errand boy's bike.

'I shan't be using the V8,' he explained. 'Mrs Gould and I will be going with your father and mother in his motor.'

Unfortunately, as I discovered, Dr Gould was even more fanatical about vehicle black-out regulations than

Father. He had masked the one permitted head-lamp so drastically that I was obliged to creep along the darkened lanes to our destination at a glow-worm's pace.

'For heaven's sake,' Alison complained, when we did eventually arrive, 'we're over an hour late.'

This was true. Whispering Harry Caldwell and his Merry Melodians were already playing the pre-supper quickstep as we made our entrance.

'Run, rabbit, run, rabbit, run, run, run,' Harry warbled. I was ready to obey Harry's instruction there and then, upon glimpsing Father's scarlet features rising out of the bowl of flowers on the VIP table behind the band. He seemed to be gesticulating at the clock on the wall.

Luckily my partner swung me into the final chorus of the quickstep before the bandleader made the announcement for refreshments.

Alison tucked into the ham sandwiches and trifle with a will.

'I'm starting on the hay in a few hours' time,' she said.

'Hay?'

'Yes. I'm in the local Land Army.'

She certainly resembled the muscular girl on the Government poster BACK TO THE LAND, although it was back to the dance floor for me.

At least Father was keeping his distance. I noticed he had accepted from Mrs Gould a paper hat of Napoleonic shape, which made his appearance even sterner than usual. This may have added to my nervousness, but it was the tango that proved my ultimate downfall. Under Harold Caldwell's baton the tempo quickened. Just as Alison was leaning into me, I heard an ominous ripping sound. In attempting the *passo doble* I had failed to notice that my heel had caught the hem of her dress.

Despite a prolonged visit to the Ladies' Room, plus Mother's offer of a safety pin, the damage proved irreparable. Dr Gould threw me a withering glance as he hurried his daughter down the steps. Mrs Gould was crying in the hall, comforted by Mother.

My own journey home, in the back of Father's car was completed in a terrible silence. Only upon reaching Resthaven did he give vent to his feelings.

'All I can say, Clara,' he said, slamming the garage doors, 'is that it's a good thing they're sending him to India. Maybe the natives won't realise what a fool he is.'

CHAPTER 21

EARLY TRAINING

My ex-serviceman's grant saw me through a law degree at Cambridge. After further study in London, I returned, a newly qualified barrister, to Wrexham, where I proceeded to explain to my parents that if I was to work from home I would need some sort of study.

'Can't think what the boy's complaining about,' was Father's comment to Mother, 'He'll find a desk already in his room. What more does he want?' No desk could possibly be squeezed into my garret on the third floor of Resthaven, so what on earth was Father talking about? I wondered.

A quick squint through the door confirmed my worst fears. The desk was nothing more than my old friend the water cistern. A large sheet of blotting paper, advertising Beechams' Pills, had been laid out on the flat-hinged top. Wedged between the cistern and the wall was a canvas gardening stool. Where my legs would go remained a mystery for me to solve, but Father obviously considered he had provided a solution to my dilemma over reference books. At the back of the cistern cover, between two large firebricks, he had placed six mildewed volumes of the *Freemasons' Guide to the Law*.

'Worshipful Brother Allington Hughes let me have them for a song,' he pointed out with pride, when I returned to the dining-room table downstairs.

'Allington Hughes has taken over his uncle's practice, he tells me. Nothing like a friendly solicitor, they say, for getting started at the Bar.' He gave his customary hiccough brought on by the Stone's ginger beer. 'Don't expect this son of yours is exactly weighed down with briefs, eh, Clara!'

Apart from an acute shortage of briefs, I had the additional problem of a total lack of transport, especially for out-of-the-way assize towns like Ruthin and Beaumaris. Neither of these was on the surviving railway line.

'I've solved that difficulty for him', Father announced the following week. We were sitting around the wireless set, well after the nine o'clock news. Carlo Carnivera and his Krazy Mandolins, from the Winter Garden, Bournemouth, seemed to have put him in a mellow mood, even delaying his normal bedtime. Mother threaded her darning needle and plunged into the the enormous mountain of Father's woollen socks.

'How have you managed that, George?' Mother was never slow to pick up a feed line.

'I've bought him a truck. Army surplus. Splendid bargain. Twenty-five pounds. With a tarpaulin cover thrown in.'

For a moment Mother looked anxious.

'Will that be quite the thing, dear? For a barrister, I mean.'

'Certainly,' came the reply. 'He's not a KC, you know. He'll be lucky to start off with a few small-time criminals.'

'But I won't actually have to drive them to court, Father' I pointed out.

'Just as well,' he said, 'you'll need all the space you've got for the pigeons.'

'*Pigeons*?'

'Yes. Pigeons. Killing two birds with one stone, you might say.'

The wartime comedy show ITMA had given him a taste for this kind of repartee.

'I've been comparing notes with Worshipful Brother Allington Hughes,' he went on. 'Apparently my pigeon-training season coincides with the Hilary Quarter Sessions. Couldn't be better.'

My precise role in Father's pigeon plans was not further defined, but no doubt this would be made clear in due course.

The Bedford fifteen hundredweight was delivered to the Resthaven garage next day. Its bodywork bore witness to a large number of serious collisions.

'Mechanically sound as a bell,' Father declared. 'All it needs is for Williams to give it a lick of paint.'

The purple-nosed Mr Williams was Father's most elderly retainer. Clad in a drooping boiler suit, he was forever dolefully engaged in giving bits of Father's property 'a lick of paint'.

Father's colours were chocolate brown and custard yellow, and this was the livery chosen for the fifteen hundredweight.

'Have you grasped the principles of pigeon training?' Father asked me, during the subsequent inspection of Mr Williams's crude handiwork.

I hesitated. 'Not really.'

'Quite simple. Each time you set out for court somewhere, you'll carry a basket of youngsters in the back.'

'Youngsters?'

'The birds that still have a lot to learn,' he snapped. 'Like you.'

Was this just another of Father's jokes? I began to ask myself. Apparently not.

'Doesn't matter where you happen to be,' he continued, 'north, south, east or west. My pigeons have to be taught to find their way back to the lofts from any direction.'

'But—'

'But nothing. All you have to do is make sure the birds are safely liberated from their baskets. Then you carry on with your court work.'

I did not have long to dwell on the implications of

father's plan. The day after the next meeting of the Square and Compass Lodge, my first brief arrived. It came from Mr Allington Hughes. I was to defend a notorious bruiser called Justin Price, for assault occasioning actual bodily harm, before the Merioneth Quarter Sessions.

After a sleepless night, bent over the water cistern, mugging up the papers, I gulped some tea in the kitchen and stumbled down to the garage. It was half-past eight and raining, but Father was already there in his galoshes.

'You'll have to store your wig and gown and briefcase at your feet,' Father said. 'There'll be no room in the back.'

One of the two benches under the rear tarpaulin was already occupied by Father's loft manager, Harold Humes. Mr Humes had a large wicker container on his knee enclosing a noisy bevy of feathered travellers.

'My things can go on the front passenger seat,' I said.

'No. That has to be kept free for Mr Allington Hughes. I told him you'd give him a lift. Save on his petrol coupons.'

I glanced in the direction of the empty bench opposite Harold Humes.

'Tommy Wynn will be sitting there. You'll be picking him up in the Station Road.'

Father explained that Mr Wynn, a collier, was a fellow member of his Fanciers' Club, the Penycae Combine, and that he would be 'helping Harold Humes to toss the fledglings'.

Half-an-hour later we were lumbering along the A5. In the back were Messrs Harold and Tommy, plus baskets. Mr Allington Hughes was seated in the front. With pigeon-racing conversation going on behind, I found it increasingly difficult to concentrate upon the legal questions fired at me by Mr Allington Hughes.

'Fine-looking hen you've got there, Harold.'

'Will you be moving to quash the indictment on the second count?'

'Lovely straight beak, has Betsy. She's my favourite. Legs a bit short though, Tommy.'

'I presume you've checked Section 17 Subsection 2(a) of the Offences Against The Person Act?'

'She'd be up against it in a head wind, Harold.'

'Judge Watkin is on the Bench today, so you'd better watch out.'

By the time we arrived at our destination, my mind was reeling. To my surprise the official parking area at Merioneth Quarter Sessions was underneath the court building.

'Pity we never stopped at Bala Lake,' said Harold Humes, as I plunged our vehicle down a concrete ramp into a subterranean passageway.

'There's no way we're going to get the buggers airborne in this bloody warren,' complained Tommy Wynn.

'It's ferrets we should be letting out here, not pigeons,' Harold agreed, 'don't know what your Dad would say. You'll have to do something about it.'

Mr Allington Hughes had already dismounted, marched round the bonnet, and opened the door on my side.

'We're already late for the pre-trial conference,' he barked.

I had no choice but to promise to return as soon as possible.

As bad luck would have it, the trial of Rex v. Justin Price was not started until after a string of bail applications. My cross-examination of the complainant, whom my client had assaulted, was of necessity a lengthy affair, and by the time I had taken Mr Price through his evidence of self-defence, the clock above Judge Watkin's grim visage was showing that three hours had elapsed.

'Where do you think *you're* going?' I overheard the usher hiss, as I was making my submissions to the jury. Out of the corner of my eye I caught sight of Harold

Humes, crouched in the aisle alongside me. It was lucky for both of us that the Judge could not see him.

From the corner of the loft manager's jacket pocket perked the indignant beak of Betsy.

'She's fair suffocating in them dungeons,' Harold whispered to me, 'and so are the rest of us.'

'Will Your Honour please grant me a short adjournment,' I stammered.

Judge Watkin frowned.

'Is nature calling?' he enquired coldly.

'Er . . . you could put it that way,' I agreed.

He turned to the twelve good men and true.

'We'll take a break of five minutes, Gentlemen of the Jury,' he said, before withdrawing to chambers.

I tore off to the Bedford, crashed it into reverse gear, and, from the adjoining police station compound, watched the fledglings soar happily in the direction of Wrexham.

Unfortunately there was a hold-up while the police station inspector issued me with a formal notice of warning for illegal parking. Judge Watkin grew tired of waiting for my return and wound up the case in my absence. I arrived back in court to discover that the defendant had gone down for six months.

'You may have successfully liberated your father's damn pigeons, young man,' declared Mr Allington Hughes. 'Pity you couldn't do the same for Mr Price!'

So that was the first and last brief I received from Mr Allington Hughes.

CHAPTER 22

THE ENGAGEMENT PARTY

'There's no getting away from it,' Mother said. 'He will have to be told.' She was referring to Father. 'What does Dr Brock think?'

'I hadn't thought of asking him,' I said.

Dr Brock was our family doctor and friend, but we were not discussing some dread illness from which Father was suffering. Merely the news that I was getting married.

'It's not going to cost him anything,' I said, 'we're going abroad.'

'He mightn't take it so badly,' interposed Aunty Carrie, 'if you were not marrying outside the Craft.' She sniffed. 'Just because the father of 'your intended' isn't one of them Freemasons! All the better, if you ask me.'

'Nobody's asking you, Miss Rogers,' said Mother.

Her pale face was showing a quite unusual anxiety.

'Well at least he's having his favourite supper tonight, Mrs Mawer,' cackled Aunty Carrie, basting the sizzling pan of fatty pork chops on the Triplex Grate. 'That might improve his temper a bit.'

The evening followed the usual pattern. At the head of the table. Father downed a vast meal with customary speed while the rest of us clustered nervously around our boiled eggs. Apart from his mandatory bout of hiccoughs after the ginger beer there was total silence throughout. He retreated to the armchair by the sitting-room fire and placed his patent leather boots on the footstool. This was the signal that the black leather slippers were required. High-sided and remarkably uncomfortable, they would only go on with the aid of a long shoe-horn, deftly manipulated by Mother.

Now, with the rest of us helping with the washing-up in the kitchen, Mother decided to broach the subject.

'You mustn't confront him,' she had warned me. 'His blood pressure's much too high for that. He could have a seizure.'

Through the gap between the hinges of the sitting room door, slightly ajar, Aunty Carrie was at her observation post. Her self-appointed task was to keep the rest of us up to date with news from the front line.

'Your mother's just handed him the *Liverpool Daily Post*,' she reported hoarsely, 'thank goodness it's the final edition and correctly folded.' Her last words were drowned in a loud cry, as of a wounded rhino.

'She's told him,' said Aunty Carrie . . .

'I've never heard anything more ridiculous in my life.' These seemed to be the only words in father's vocabulary for the next week. Occasionally, to add weight to his objections, the name of a mystic ally was invoked, in the shape of one Tommy Dewar. Tommy Dewar was the only barrister known to father. He was the Lecturer in Forensic Pharmacy to the Pharmaceutical Society.

'The earliest age for a barrister to contemplate marriage is 45. How many times do I have to repeat what Tommy Dewar has told me?'

'But Ronnie says he's going abroad in the Colonial Legal Service, dear,' Mother repeated.

'The subject is closed,' came the reply . . .

The next move in the crisis was made by my future mother-in-law, a lady of resolute vivacity. Hatted and gloved in the style of the late 1940s, she conferred with other leading Wrexham socialites over morning coffee at Stevens's High Class Café in Hope Street.

'Since these two young people seem to have quite made

up their minds,' she informed Father over the telephone, 'Frank and I are giving a little cocktail party for them.'

'I'm afraid cocktail parties are not my cup of tea,' she was told sternly.

'Then that's exactly what you can have, Mr Knox Mawer, a cup of tea,' came the reply.

Father was foxed.

'I see, I see, quite. Quite.'

He replaced the receiver after a mumbled exchange of politenesses. Father was never discourteous when cornered.

There was no mention of Mother. It had been made universally clear, over 35 years, that, apart from the August holiday, father was never accompanied anywhere by Mrs Knox Mawer. Nevertheless it was Mother whom he now summoned urgently to discuss this latest development.

'Clara,' he called, 'where on earth are you?'

Mother peered down the cellar steps.

'What is it, George?' she wanted to know.

The siting of the telephone, in the cellar, was an idea of Father's. He believed that the extreme difficulty of negotiating the steep descent would 'stop those children of yours wasting phone calls.' Knowing that every bill was scrutinised minutely by him, we should never have dreamed of making a call, so the only person at risk was Father himself.

'Very grave news indeed,' Father gasped, as he emerged breathless through the cellar door. 'It looks as though things are getting out of hand. I shall have to put my thinking cap on.'

Presumably he must have been wearing this symbolic headgear at the next Lodge Night; my betrothal was obviously the subject of animated discussion in King Solomon's Temple, Colliery Road.

'I'm told the Worshipful Master is attending this-this

"engagement party",' he informed Mother, upon his return. He snapped the rear stud out of his wing collar. 'Puts me in an awkward position, most awkward.'

The reigning Worshipful Master of the Square and Compass Lodge was Mr Noel Parry, a local accountant, well known for his sociability. 'Living in the Cocktail Belt,' as father put it grimly.

This Masonic connection had given the saga an unexpected twist. Father had no alternative but to reconsider the invitation.

* * *

'I should like to propose a toast to the newly engaged couple,' announced Mr Parry. The party was just getting into its swing.

'Hold on a minute, Noel,' interrupted Percy Horton, a prosperous Wrexham jeweller.

Mr Horton, glass in hand, was standing in the bow window of my fiancée's home. He had spotted the familiar brown and yellow Army truck shuddering to a halt at the bottom of the steep tarmac drive.

'It's Mr Knox Mawer's pigeon van,' exclaimed another guest knowledgeably. We all crowded to the window.

'I knew he'd come,' said our hostess in some triumph.

As she went to welcome the late-comer, the rest of us watched Father go to the back of the vehicle and lift up the tarpaulin cover.

'Maybe he's brought a dove of peace!' suggested Percy Horton, the wit of the Cocktail Belt.

'It looks like a plant,' corrected my fiancée, 'how awfully sweet of him. I'm sure he's not the ogre he's made out to be.' She dashed out to join her mother on the front step.

'We're so glad you've come. Just in time to toast the happy couple,' Father was told.

'What will you have to drink?'

Father was busy wedging an enormous cactus between the umbrellas in the front porch, a present for his hosts, apparently.

'*Cactus, gloriosus*', he said.

'I'm afraid we don't have any,' faltered the lady of the house, 'What about a drop of whisky?'

Father looked startled. 'Nothing to drink,' he declared.

A few niceties were exchanged on the doorstep but Father could not be persuaded to venture any further onto the premises. His expression suggested that a plague cross must be marked on the door.

The sound of clinking glasses and laughter floated out from the lounge as snow began to fall. Father, meanwhile, was peering hard at an outside pipe, then poked at the ice with his walking stick.

'You've got a blocked drain there,' were his parting words, as he retreated down the drive.

'I can see that that girl he is marrying will be most expensive on make-up, Clara,' he observed, when safely back in Resthaven, 'but her mother tells me she obtained a distinction in her Higher School Certificate.'

He brought out three ten pound bank notes, counted them carefully, replaced one in his wallet, and passed two across the table.

'So tell the wretched boy to buy her a decent ring. That cheap item I noticed upon her finger is a positive disgrace.'

CHAPTER 23

WEDDING BELLS

'A Festival of Britain indeed,' Father snorted, lashing at a bluebottle with his *Daily Mail*. 'Festival of Bankruptcy more like.'

It was 1947 and Mr Attlee was planning ahead for a break in the cloud of austerity.

'I shall have to write a letter of complaint.'

Complaining, to Father, was a way of life. For almost two decades we children had provided him with a major source of complaint material. Everything we did at 26 Grosvenor Road seemed to goad him beyond endurance.

'They're nothing but a load of millstones around my neck, Clara,' was his constant cry.

The all-engrossing challenge now, therefore, was how to rid himself of the millstones as rapidly as possible.

'I don't know why I took them on in the first place,' he would add, as though we were a consignment of substandard goods that had been dumped with him by an artful commercial traveller.

Where I was concerned the solution was comparatively simple — an appointment to some remote outpost of Empire. As he frequently pointed out, the indigenous folk would be rather more tolerant of my short-comings than my fellow countrymen.

My sisters, however, were a more complicated proposition.

'Don't most daughters get married, for heaven's sake?' I heard him demand of Mother. 'The Worshipful Master had no difficulty with his girl.'

'Myra Watkin-Powell wasn't exactly a girl, dear,' Mother demurred. 'As far as I remember, she was nearly forty.'

Mother looked fondly at the three pallid faces of her female progeny squeezed together in the Kodak Brownie give-away frame on the side-board.

'Ours are only in their teens, George.'

'Passive resistance again, Clara. You seem to be deliberately encouraging them to hang about the place.'

'Rosemary's still at school,' Mother added as an afterthought.

'It's never too soon to think ahead,' was Father's riposte.

He retreated to the chair with his pharmaceutical jotting pad, headed IRON JELLOIDS FOR NERVOUS ENERGY.

For some days Father buried himself with drawing up a list of potential suitors. The resulting selection was a testimony to his taste for the bizarre.

All unmarried curates in the Wrexham diocese were listed and catalogued, those of Low Church persuasion attracting a star of merit. Then came all new entrants to the Masonic Order who were of bachelor status. The star here was awarded to Gordon Stephenson, secretary of the Square and Compass Lodge, whose bicycle clips, enormous ears, and prematurely balding head had already attracted our attention. There was also Mr Eli Humphreys, a lugubrious chemist in Colwyn Bay specialising in gentlemen's appliances.

At this point, Father's attention was mercifully diverted to another fruitful source of complaint — Major Herford Jenkins and the manure. The list was put away for the time being, on the spike for bills in the study.

Not surprisingly, in the course of time, my sisters made their own choice — very poor ones, Father thought, but he drew some comfort from the fact that the weddings took place in rapid succession. He had always preferred to deal in bulk and endeavoured, without success, to negotiate an overall fee with the vicar. Fortunately the continuance of Government food rationing meant that utility receptions were the order of the day. Our dining-room table turned out to be an expanding one. With the aid of a heavy cranking handle, Mr Humes laboriously inserted the two leaves but was smartly ordered by Father to take them out again.

'There's nothing expansive about this affair,' he remarked to Mother, 'although I've been pretty liberal over the liquid refreshments.'

We brightened at this news — until the six large crates, delivered the next afternoon, turned out to be Dr Metcalfe's Tonic Wine. The menu was what Father termed a cold collation. His last carton of wartime corned beef, retrieved from the cellar, formed the cornerstone of the repast. Consequently — with life imitating art in its usual way — several guests were forcibly reminded of Father's famous advertisement for his indigestion mixture in the *North Wales Guardian*, headed FEELING ILL IN WREXHAM?

Two weddings down and one to go, the day approached for him to give away my youngest sister. Father grew noticeably more cheerful.

'At least I'll have the last of them off my hands, Clara,' he observed. 'That fool of a boy as well.' He was referring to the fact that soon after Rosemary's wedding I was expecting to take up a post in the Colonial Service. But about three weeks before the final nuptials it suddenly dawned upon Father that life was going to be unpleasantly carefree without the millstones. It seemed that he would need to discover some fresh adversity with which to occupy himself. The trouble was where to find a really long-term source of trial and tribulation, especially now that he had retired from the business.

Inspiration came, as it usually did, while he was carving the Sunday roast. The carving knife was poised over the knuckle of the leg of lamb which was traditionally apportioned to me.

'We have a grave problem, Clara,' he suddenly announced.

He shot one of his warning glances, over his new horn-rimmed spectacles, around the table, before picking up the steel to resharpen the knife.

'Financial Ruin,' he declared in between strokes. 'With all the expense of these weddings I'm a ruined man.'

The carving completed, Father sat down and unrolled his freshly starched napkin with a flourish.

'There's nothing else for it. We shall have to take in lodgers.'

As the meal proceeded, Father warmed to his theme. A whole range of emergency measures would be necessary if Resthaven was to be transformed into a source of income and the spectre of destitution kept at bay.

'Miss Rogers can easily manage any extra washing,' he asserted, helping himself to a large dollop of onion sauce. He seemed oblivious to the fact that Aunty Carrie, now 89 and crippled with arthritis, had long since retired to a cottage on the River Dee. A laundry boy had been calling at Resthaven for the last five years. Perhaps Father had taken him for 'one of those wretched ner-do-wells,' as he described the occasional friend of mine brave enough to call on me at home.

'I shall need to spend some time in the study drawing a plan for the alterations,' he declared at the end of the main course.

'Alterations?' echoed Mother, who up till then had remained speechless like the rest of us.

'Accommodation will naturally be self-contained. The house will have to be divided in two. I'm not having perfect strangers living cheek by jowl with me, for goodness sake!'

I imagined the strangers themselves would have even stronger views about such proximity to Father.

Another silence fell while Father demolished his apple pie and custard in a few swift spoonfuls and rose from the table.

'The work must be set in hand immediately.'

Within days, a programme of Bulk Deliveries was set in motion.

'Couldn't some of it wait until after the wedding reception, dear?' Mother enquired, peering desperately through the French window as the latest load of building material was unloaded on the drive. Father had disposed of his livestock to Worshipful Brother Bowman. Now every corner of the garden bulged with scaffolding, pipes, bricks and tiles. Bags of cement and several heaps of sand severely restricted the use of both front and back doors. The rose garden was now occupied by two lavatory units and one large enamel bath.

'Time waits for no man,' came the inevitable rejoinder. Rosemary burst into tears and disappeared into her bedroom. 'Wedding nerves already,' Father observed breezily. 'Remind me to bring her a bottle of Vita-calm yeast tonic tomorrow.'

My sister was in need of more than one bottle by the time the great day dawned.

'Isn't it time you went upstairs to change, dear?' Mother ventured. The service at the parish church was scheduled for midday. Father however was still wearing his gardening coat, one of his discarded mackintoshes.

'I'm not sure that Percy Edge can do without me,' he replied.

Mr Edge was Father's building contractor — a carpenter-cum-bricklayer-cum-plumber, and husband of the faithful Edith — who at that very moment was at the top of a ladder knocking out a brick for the insertion of an outlet pipe.

'If I'm still needed to hold these steps I can see no alternative but to remain at my post. This boy will simply have to deputise for me.'

'What on earth will the family think, George?' Mother expostulated.

'The family will think I'm helping Mr Edge with the plumbing, that's what they'll think. And they'll be quite right.'

'But Ronnie is the Best Man, Father,' protested my sister.

'Worst Man, you mean,' he chaffed, repeating his joke of the month for the twenty-sixth time that week.

In fact he had not the remotest intention of abrogating his parental duty. He merely liked to create an air of suspense. Punctual to the dot, he arrived at the church with my sister on his arm.

The wedding service went off without a hitch, although with Father standing at such close quarters, the vicar became so nervous that he twice forgot his lines. In his confusion, I though at one moment he was going to marry Father to Mrs Jarvis Roberts, who was leaning forward tremulously in the front row, resplendent in a hat like a flowered coal-scuttle.

A steady drizzle fell upon the tiny motorcade wending its way from the church gates back to 26 Grosvenor Road. Father sat bolt upright in the front of Isaac Jones's convertible wedding/funeral limousine. White ribbons cost extra, and in his hour of need Father had dispensed with them as an unnecessary luxury. He was wearing a heavy black morning coat, black top hat, black waistcoat and black tie, so it was understandable that a short-sighted passer-by doffed his cap when the cortège passed by.

The drive up to Resthaven had become a quagmire.

'What about a few duck-boards?' suggested Colonel Jarvis Roberts, a Flanders veteran of the First World War.

But Father and Percy Edge were already setting up a walkway of planks.

Nearly everybody negotiated the crossing safely. Only Uncle Ted had to be helped out and offered a change of clothing. For Father this was the highlight of the day.

'Do the fellow good,' he was heard to remark between chuckles.

His good humour lasted him right up to his speech, which was particularly mellow in tone. After five minutes he was in full swing.

'My message to these two young people,' he continued, a slight glaze upon his features after another large gulp of tonic wine, 'in voyaging on the sea of matrimony is to expect Rough Weather. Indeed I would go further, and say welcome to the stormy waves. Batten down your hatches and weather the Gales of Life together. Holy wedlock cannot be tested in calm seas alone.'

He leaned forward and fixed his gaze upon Mother who looked up nervously.

'Clara here will be the first to testify that the solid foundations of our happy hearth and home are based upon a constant readiness to give and take. She has her foibles. Indeed I may have one or two of my own. But the secret of a happy domestic life is tolerance.' A murmur of surprise ran through the gathering which Father ignored.

'I have not a bit of time,' he declaimed, 'for the street saint and home sinner. Eve, we are told, was fashioned out of the rib of Adam. But that does not give Adam the right to rule the roost. Far from it.' He cleared his throat. 'And when in the course of time you reach the sunset years you will both be able to look out, look back upon the years of understanding, one to the other and back again.'

Emotion seemed to be running high. He paused to

draw out a handkerchief. Somebody started to clap, but Father continued.

'A touch of the hand in times of stress, a smile of encouragement in the face of woe.'

He seemed to be wandering, then pulled himself together.

'Say not the struggle nought availeth,' be boomed mysteriously, 'for eastward look the land is bright.'

Father had chosen to deliver his address from a clearing in the rubble where Mr Edge was dismantling the Victorian hall fireplace for his central heating plant. We the congregation were bunched around the speaker in various contorted positions of discomfort.

'Er, no,' Father corrected himself '*westward* look the land is bright.'

We followed the direction of his outstretched finger. Out of the wasteland of his building operations, there appeared the stricken figure of Mr Edge at the french window. He was clutching his hair and mouthing some urgent message through the glass. At the same moment the reverberations of Father's oratory gave way to a high-pitched droning sound, coming from the fireplace.

Mr Edge managed to wrench open the window. At close quarters his face was seen to be curiously red and swollen.

'It's the bees, sir,' he cried, 'the little buggers have swarmed in the chimney!'

The humming grew in volume and there was an instant retreat by the guests from the vicinity of the fireplace.

'No cause for panic,' Father declared. He held up a calming hand.

'This is a fortuitous example of one of those testing points in life about which I happen to have been speaking. The key word is resourcefulness.'

He turned to the bride.

'Rosemary,' he said, 'Kindly hand me your veil.'

'But, George,' Mother began.

'But nothing, Clara. Where's that boy?'

He jerked round in my direction.

'Go and fetch the sweeping rods from the shed.'

By the time I returned with the equipment, the guests had fled to the garden. The room was empty save for a spectral figure with head and face swathed in white tulle, crouched by the fireplace.

'I'll have the queen and her entourage trapped in next to no time,' a muffled voice declared, manoeuvring a large sack into position around the mouth of the fireplace.

The humming was now at fever pitch. Mr Humes was despatched to the roof with the rods and brushes, and I retreated to the rose garden, administering the blue-bag amongst the guests wherever necessary, along with plenty of tonic wine.

Rosemary and the groom retired upstairs to change. A peremptory toot from Mr Isaac Jones, at the front gate, reminded them that they were due to catch the 4.10 from Paddington. Framed in the side door, the couple emerged in their going-away clothes. Family and friends picked their way through the debris to see them on their way.

'An unforgettable day, Mrs Mawer,' said Mother's new son-in-law.

From the roof, where Harold Humes had positioned himself, there came an ominous sound of dislodgement. A thin shower of soot began to fall, mingling with the confetti.

Rosemary was giving Mother a farewell kiss when a strange, dusky figure loomed up behind them, only recognisable by the glint of his spectacles.

'Goodbye and good luck, my dear,' said Father.

An approving hum emanated from the tightly knotted sock in his right hand. It was at this point that that Mr Jenkins stepped forward to snap the happy scene for posterity.

Mr Jenkins' photograph never fails to arouse interest. Who is the exotic stranger in a tattered white turban? I am asked. How can I explain? Nobody believes me when I tell them that it is just another example of Father 'dealing with one of life's little challenges'.

CHAPTER 24

FAREWELL TO FATHER

As a Colonial Legal Probationer I was training in chambers in Liverpool for my first posting.

'You will kindly proceed to Aden forthwith,' Whitehall notified me.

My ship was to sail in a week's time. There was no putting off the farewell encounter with Father. I walked up from the Wrexham General station and into the familiar road. Nothing seemed to have changed — Ivy Toft School, the Roman Catholic Convent, and Major Herford Jenkins lurking behind the hedge with his clippers.

As I opened the gate of Number 26, the Misses Johnson peeped out from under the faded Victorian sunblinds of Number 28. They had traditionally taken an interest in my comings and goings. Every Good Friday I used to be sent by Father to their turreted fastness with what he called a Spring Bulb.

'What do you think it is this year, Emily?,' the smaller sister would ask, holding the long, drooping plant in the purple bowl at arm's length.

'Perhaps it's hoping to be a narcissus, Katherine.'

'Never mind, dear,' Miss Emily would say, handing me a sixpence, 'it's the thought that counts.'

I had to deposit the sixpence in my Midland Bank money box, a diabolical contrivance designed to keep the coin inside for ever.

'Only the bank manager's got the key,' Aunty Carrie used to cackle, watching my futile efforts to extract the sixpence when Father had departed for the shop.

I rang the familiar rusty bell of Resthaven. It gave out the usual flat note. I was gazing round at the neatly restored drive as footsteps approached and the door was opened.

'Hello there, Edith,' I said.

'I beg yerr pardon!' replied a Scottish bass voice.

I turned to face a tall gingery gentleman in a kilt.

'Oh, sorry, I expected the housemaid,' I said.

'I'm sorry to disappoint you laddie. The name's McPherson, Captain Angus McPherson. I'm tenanting the upstairs flat.'

Father's conversion of Resthaven had obviously proceeded at lightning speed.

'The landlord,' McPherson growled 'resides on the ground floor at the rear of the building. And the less we see of him the better. Had I realised what an impossible man he is, we should certainly not have taken on a twelve month lease. My wife Jennie's on the brink of a nervous breakdown.'

'I'm sorry you've had a bit of trouble,' I said, feeling more than a touch of fellow sympathy.

I tried a joke.

'How long have you done so far?'

'Precisely one month,' snapped the Captain, 'and it seems like a life sentence already!'

I thought it was high time I made my own position clear.

'I'm sorry to say you're speaking about my father.'

'Then I'm very sorry for you,' he replied, closing the door firmly in my face.

I made my way to the side of the house but was stopped in my tracks by a new wooden fence festooned with Father's barbed wire. The old notice board, which had formerly said 'Tradesmen's Entrance,' had been daubed out. Underneath, in shaky black lettering — obviously the work of old Mr Ashley, were the words MR AND MRS G R KNOX MAWER AT HOME.

For as long as I could remember, Mr Ashley had been employed at Resthaven as a kind of resident painter. On this occasion he was not restricted to the usual varnish-brush, and there were only three obvious spelling alterations.

As a final touch, Mr Ashley had attempted a pointing hand with a finger in red paint, extending vaguely in the direction of the dust-bins. Let into the fence further along was a wicket gate. After a struggle with the latch I emerged on the other side.

'Anybody at home?' I called.

Mother's anxious face peeped over the Ruabon brick that surrounded the back yard — forever associated in my mind with one of Father's most devastating tantrums. At that time (1935) it had been paved in ridged Victorian tiles of leaden hue, most of them broken and as dangerous as a minefield. In Father's absence, at the pharmaceutical conference, Mr Humes and I had been seized by a wild impulse to improve things. When Father returned, the area was covered with a neat layer of concrete. His eyes nearly popped out of his head. Thundering and flailing like a man possessed, he cornered Mr Humes with his brief case and umbrella and accused him of 'destroying the finest back yard in North Wales'. I was crouched like a rabbit in the doorway of the woodshed when Father turned upon me. He grabbed me by the ear, thrust me inside and bolted the door behind him..

'Vandals,' I heard him bellow as he went indoors, 'no sense of history whatsoever . . . priceless heritage . . . irreplaceable.'

It was across that infamous square of concrete that Mother now beckoned me.

'So glad you found time to call, dear,' she whispered. 'Come inside. We don't want to disturb your father.'

She threw a warning glance in the direction of the wash-house. Steam was emerging from under its ill-fitting stable door, which remained unchanged from Father's building operations.

'What's he doing?' I asked, 'he's not taken over Aunty Carrie's job, has he?' Mother giggled nervously.

'No dear. He's taking a bath.'

As I stared at the tiny misted window a large hand appeared, rubbing it clear. This was followed by an irritable scarlet face.

'If it's that boy,' Father called out, 'tell him the fire's gone out in this boiler. As soon as I'm out of here, the hose-pipe will be needed for draining off.'

He disappeared again and Mother drew me hastily indoors.

'Surely you don't go out there to have a bath as well, Mother!' I exclaimed.

'It's not too bad,' she said mildly, 'so long as it doesn't freeze.'

After a few minutes Father joined us in the breakfast room. He was as immaculately dressed as ever, from the starched white prongs of his wing collar to the polished caps of his black boots. He gave me a brisk nod.

'The hose-pipe is in its usual place. Make sure it's tied up neatly when you've finished it.' He turned to Mother. 'A bit of exercise will do the boy good, Clara. He's looking very peaky, cooped up in those dusty lawyers' rooms all day.'

'Ronnie's called to say goodbye, George,' Mother ventured. 'He's sailing from Tilbury next Thursday.'

Father heaved an exasperated sigh.

'Well I suppose I could get Humes to sluice out in the morning,' he said.

'I'm glad you've still got Mr Humes to give you a hand,' I said, 'how are you managing generally?'

'Poverty's staring me in the face, I'm afraid,' Father

replied. 'I've had to double the wage of the loft manager, while Humes himself is demanding an overtime rate. And now there's the chauffeur to pay.'

'Chauffeur,' I thought. 'Had Father completely lost his senses?'

'Two pounds to Evan Griffiths every time I want to go anywhere in the car. He must think he's still running that Crosville double decker of his.'

'Mr Griffiths is a retired bus driver in Vernon Street,' Mother explained. 'Father's phlebitis has been playing up a bit, so Mr Griffiths is glad to supplement his pension.'

Mother's own daily help had laid out a kind of high tea, obviously part of Father's economy regime — bread and margarine, bloater paste and seedcake. We sat down by the recently installed fireplace. This was an offensive sausage colour —Father's choice — and had taken the place of the old-fashioned triplex grate.

Mother broke the customary silence.

'Your father has just returned from the Freemasons' Hall in London. A meeting of the Masonic VIPs wasn't it, George?'

Father was busily inspecting a dish of stewed gooseberries brought in by Mother, to ensure that they had been correctly topped and tailed.

'As a matter of fact,' he observed, 'I happened to have a very useful conversation there with the Grand Warden.'

He jerked forward irritably.

'Here's one you've missed, Clara!'

He thrust out a slightly squashed gooseberry, at the same time knocking over the custard jug. Mother neatly fielded both items and retreated into the kitchen.

'We were talking about this boy, as a matter of fact, Clara,' Father continued, addressing Mother's empty chair in the usual way. 'The Grand Warden happens to be Sir Sidney Abrahams, the top man in the Colonial Legal Service.'

I quailed inwardly. 'Quite a coincidence, Father,' I said. 'Sounds as if this job in Aden is just the ticket.'

Father's unfamiliar note of enthusiasm was oddly disturbing. Perhaps he was mellowing in his retirement, I thought. But no.

'Sir Sidney tells me the Indian Army used Aden as a punishment station,' Father went on. 'He says it's got the worst climate in the Empire. Nothing to do there but your duty — keeping law and order among the Arab tribes. A garrison life on the barren desert rocks. Altogether an excellent training ground for the ambitious young colonial recruit!'

Father met my eye for the first time, and delivered one of his typical non-sequiturs.

'You'd better make use of my new convenience,' he said, 'your colour's much too pasty.'

'Just to please him,' Mother urged, 'he's rather proud of it.'

I could see nothing convenient about the converted Andersen air-raid shelter in the far corner of the vegetable garden. For reasons best known to Father, a Mickey Mouse alarm clock was propped up on an adjoining ledge. In the interests of economy, he had made good use of the *Chemist and Druggist* Information Pamphlets 1921–25, hanging on a nail neatly threaded through a piece of gardening twine.

I came out to find Father sitting with Mother in the rose garden. They seemed to be having a private *tête-a-tête* about me, so I tactfully concealed myself behind the rustic woodwork that supported the Aberconway Ramblers.

'A good thing, Clara, that we've heard no more nonsense from this boy about getting married.'

Mother was wearing one of her worried looks.

'Ronnie's fiancé is following him out there, George. They're going to be married in the garrison church.'

Father slapped a hand to his forehead.

'Is there no end to the boy's stupidity! It's common knowledge that an officer in the Colonial Service does not marry during his first tour of duty. Bound to doom his career from the start.'

'But surely, George,' Mother began.

'But surely nothing, Clara. Cold showers and regular exercise are what he should be thinking about.'

There was a pause.

'Damned weed,' I heard him explode.

This was a novel epithet as far as I was concerned. It was time to stand up for myself and face the music. When I emerged, however, Father was merely tugging up a large dandelion from between the paving stones.

'Harold Humes is slacking again,' he complained.

'I gather you're discussing my wedding,' I broke in defiantly. 'It's a pity that neither of you will be there. But we'll certainly be sending you plenty of photographs.'

Father turned to Mother.

'What does the boy say?'

At first I imagined he was becoming a little deaf. Upon close observation, though, I realised that he had deftly slipped into position a pair of his Swedish earplugs. These he had taken to keeping in his waistcoat pocket for instant use where something irritating was said for which he had no ready reply.

Mother tried to repeat what I had told them, but Father had already found something to divert his attention. He glared in the direction of the orchard.

'She's done it again, Clara,' he announced.

Father pointed an indignant finger at a small clothesline discreetly slung between the two pear trees behind the rockery. Mrs McPherson had hung out a few small towels and pillowslips to dry in the breeze.

'It's another blatant contravention of the tenancy agreement,' Father continued.

He sprang up from the seat we had been sharing in the rose arbour.

'I shall take it up with them immediately.'

'But, George,' Mother protested, 'you've taken up three different complaints with Captain McPherson already today.'

'Then another one might bring the man to his senses,' Father rejoined.

He started off up the main gravel path.

'Do try and dissuade him, Ronnie,' Mother urged.

I caught up with him by the new notice board.

'It's a question of principle. Some people will do anything for peace and quiet. That's not my style, thank goodness.'

He strode out of the gate and disappeared with his walking stick in the direction of the front door. It was clear that Father was savouring this latest struggle for power. His theatre of war had expanded to two fronts. There was the continuing feud with Major Herford Jenkins to the south, and now these invigorating daily clashes with Captain McPherson on the northern frontier.

With an air of a job well done, Father eventually returned to his side of the fence.

'That's game, set and match,' he declared, swinging his walking stick like a tennis racquet.

'Perhaps we should have them down for a cup of tea in the rose garden tomorrow, George,' Mother said. It was her ingrained habit to pour oil on troubled waters. 'To talk over these little differences, I mean.' I could see Father was about to explode again, so I tried to intervene.

'Well I'll be saying cheerio,' I said. 'Must get back to Liverpool to start packing up my flat.'

But Father's eye was now fixed on the upper storey of the house.

'They've not had the windows cleaned, you know, Clara,' he barked, 'despite what I told them on Sunday afternoon.' Whipping out his pharmaceutical diary he was making notes for the next encounter.

Mother put her hand on his arm.

'You won't be seeing Ronnie for a couple of years, dear, you know.'

'I don't know what the world's coming to,' Father said, absentmindedly shaking my hand.

I thought that I'd seen the last of Father until my first leave. My main luggage had already gone off in a brass-bound trunk (insect-proof) to the docks at Tilbury for loading on to the P & O *Mooltan*. The Colonial Office sent me a single railway ticket from Rockferry.

With my blue barrister's bag on the hat rack above my head, I was relaxing in the unaccustomed luxury of a First Class compartment, complete with white antimacassars and padded arm-rests, when the Paddington train stopped at Wrexham General.

'I trust you've also booked me a seat in the dining car as instructed, Guard,' an all-too familiar voice boomed out from the corridor.

It seemed that fate had decreed that Father was to have me under his eye to the bitter end. A red face glared at me through the glass, eyes staring. Father was obviously as put out as I was. He pulled out his pocket-watch to cover his confusion.

'Three minutes late,' he said.

'Sorry, Father,' I replied, out of habit.

'Quite a coincidence,' he muttered with a frown, settling himself down on the other side of the compartment.

Father did not like coincidences. They interfered with his system of planning ahead as sole arbiter of his own and everyone else's fate. It seemed there had been an unexpected summons to London for an emergency meeting of the Pharmaceutical Council. He had had no idea that I would be making the journey at the same time and he was at pains to make clear that no kind of surprise send-off was intended.

'Of course not, Father,' I reassured him.

With an air of relief he unfolded his copy of *The Times*.

As we sped through the Border countryside I studied the sepia photographs of holiday resorts ranged above his head. In the centre was a familiar view of the Newquay beaches. 'TRAVEL TO SUNNY CORNWALL BY GREAT WESTERN', read the caption. If only Father had accepted this invitation all those summers ago. Crouched in the back seat of the Clyno fighting the deadly car-sickness, how I used to envy the smiling children in the brown and cream coaches as they glided smoothly past on the line that ran parallel with the road over Bodmin Moor! Donald Rathwell's family always went on holiday by train. His prize trophy, I recalled, was the Trainspotters Notebook, crammed with a splendid collection of famous engine numbers.

My reverie was interrupted by the head waiter sliding open our compartment door.

'Kindly take your seats for lunch in the diner, gentlemen,' he said.

'I'll be right along, Albert,' Father responded.

Albert, in his brown braided trousers, brown mess jacket, and lapels embroidered GWR, handed Father the menu card.

'If you're sharing my table, don't forget that I have to sit with my back to the locomotive.'

'I've brought sandwiches and a flask, thank you,' I demurred.

This demonstration of economy appealed to Father. With an approving nod he disappeared down the corridor.

From Wolverhampton to Coventry, I had the compartment to myself. I would have dozed off if only the canvas blinds could have been persuaded to remain in place.

They seemed designed to spring back the moment I closed my eyes, letting in a blaze of sunshine. In exasperation I tugged at the leather strap, flung down the window and leaned out for a breath of air. At this moment a fragment of soot flew into my eye, causing it to water copiously. I was fumbling for something to stem the tears streaming down my face when Father appeared in the doorway. He cleared his throat.

'Suppose it's been a trying occasion for you, bidding farewell to this young lady of yours at Liverpool,' he said gruffly.

He was much relieved when I pointed out the true nature of my problem.

'Hold still!' he commanded.

In a trice he whipped out his starched white handkerchief. The corner was licked and the foreign body flicked away with the same expertise he had displayed on our only other train journey together. That was a day excursion to Rhyl in 1931, a reward for being top in arithmetic. Part of the package on that occasion had been a ginger pop.

As if reading my thoughts, Father reached into his jacket pocket, and produced a bottle of Wrexham Sparkling Ginger (Ginger Ales, the Wine of Wales).

'Perhaps you'd care for this,' he said. 'Albert's removed the top, so you won't need your opener.' I should have known better than to ask, but I was curious.

'What opener?'

'Don't tell me you're travelling without your Baden-Powell!'

As we drew into Paddington Station, all came back to me. On my eighth birthday, Father had enrolled me in the Masonic Children's Wolf-Cubs. He followed this up with a present of a Baden-Powell scouting knife. The instrument had two rather blunt blades, a bottle opener, a primitive compass, and a strange spike for the extraction of stones from horses' hooves (never put to the test).

I was reluctant to admit that I had immediately swopped it for Donald Rathwell's mouth organ. Each time the front door of Resthaven closed upon Father's back, I proceeded to drive the rest of the family insane with my own arrangement of 'Tiger Rag'. Old habits die hard.

'I'm afraid I mislaid it,' I apologised. 'It was seventeen years ago,' I added in mitigation.

The porter had already removed Father's luggage onto the platform.

'Just the three suitcases is it, sir?'

'That's right,' Father told him. 'Travelling light, only up for forty-eight hours.'

We parted at the ticket barrier. Father was catching a taxi to the Hotel Russell — home from home, as he called it, which certainly put the place in a class of its own. I had to find my connection for Tilbury.

He joined the throng of passengers making for the cab rank.

'Good luck,' he called back chaffingly. 'You'll certainly need it if you find yourself stranded in the desert without your Baden-Powell.'

I watched the slate-grey trilby bob above the porter's head. It seemed impossible for Father to melt into a crowd, with his outdated Victorian dress and stiff, commanding stride. As usual he gave the impression of being totally oblivious of those around him. To me, however, he looked curiously vulnerable in his isolation, especially now that he was showing his age. Then he became smaller in the distance that now separated us.

Without knowing it was the last time I was to see him, I realised that what I felt for him, against all the odds, was love.

CHAPTER 25

LET TRIBULATION ABOUND

'Why the Almighty God doesn't consult me about things, I can never understand.'

This was one of Father's familiar reproofs, delivered whenever he was particularly exasperated by the latest turn of events in world affairs or personal matters.

At the end of his life, did the Great Reaper comply, I wonder, by seeking Father's opinion on the most important question of all? Was Father asked to choose his own point of departure from the world?

If so, his response must have been clear and to the point.

'Sitting in my own chair, of course.'

It was from the chair, in his last summer (1959), that Father had frequently been minded to recite a favourite adage.

'If a job's worth doing, it's worth doing well.'

The recipient was Harold Humes, who, under Father's supervision, was laboriously repairing what Father called the rustic archways in the rose garden. Apparently Father's drive to improve things remained undiminished.

The early days of September saw him in excellent health. On the first Sunday in the month he enjoyed his customary weekend argument with Major Herford Jenkins. Dental surgeon Herford Jenkins was of altogether stouter fibre than Father's other foe, Captain McPherson, who had long since departed the field of battle.

The Major was objecting again to the obtrusive height of Father's compost heap by the party wall. Father countered with a vigorous invention about a smell from the Major's goldfish pond. The exchange ended as usual in a gratifying stalemate.

Father's mind was much diverted in the following week masterminding the five-hour rehearsal for the Masonic initiation of the assistant town clerk to the Square and Compass Lodge. He also lost a satisfying number of pigeon races.

At 1.55 p.m. on September 9th, he took his seat in the Chair. He had eaten what he called a cold collation, otherwise known to Mother as the end of the joint, with beetroot from the garden in pharmaceutical vinegar from the shop. Mother switched on the two o'clock news and placed his crystallised-ginger near to hand. She then slipped out to take a cake from the oven. Some minutes later she happened to pass the sitting-room door again. The wireless was still on, and a woman's voice was giving detailed instructions on how to cope with the menopause. Mildly suprised — *Woman's Hour* was a programme Father invariably snapped off before it hardly began — Mother hastened into the room, cloth in hand. She discovered Father with his eyes firmly closed. He sometimes took a nap after lunch. This time he was not to be roused. Dr Brock was summoned.

'A wonderful way to go,' he pronounced, 'cerebral stroke. No warning. No pain.'

At least that was a comforting thought, Mother told me. I had flown home from Arabia immediately upon receiving her telegram. Now we were sitting together on the sofa looking at the empty chair. The jar of ginger was still at the ready.

'Just about the only pleasure he admitted to,' she said fondly.

Pleasure was not what life for Father had been about.

Some explanation of his philosophy was provided by the Midland Bank, Wrexham. In Father's safe deposit was found a rare volume, bound in calf, on the life of John Knox, 1505 to 1572. It had been given to him by his grandparents who greatly revered the dour injunctions of the thundering Scot, an ancestor on the distaff side.

His early upbringing had been largely in their hands, since his own papa, Captain Robert, liked to have his pretty young wife, Father's mother, with him at sea. These grandparents had taught him that earthly existence was a grim obstacle race. The follies of life must be rejected in favour of icy linoleum, endless toil, and coal tar soap.

When Father became President of the Pharmaceutical Society of Great Britain, it was suggested to him that he should apply for a coat-of-arms. Had he done so, there is no doubt what his choice of motto would have been. He would simply have given the title of this calfbound family book – *Let tribulation abound*.

84 CHARING CROSS ROAD

Helene Hanff

'Unmitigated delight from cover to cover' *Daily Telegraph*

First published in the UK in 1971, 84 CHARING CROSS ROAD has now become something of a classic, more recently increasing its wide circle of fans when it was seen in a London stage adaptation. It is the very simple story of the love affair between Miss Helene Hanff of New York and Messrs Marks and Co, sellers of rare and secondhand books, at 84 Charing Cross Road, London.

'Immensely appealing . . . witty, caustic' *Listener*

'20 years of faithful and uproarious correspondence with a bookshop in Charing Cross Road' *Evening Standard*

'A lovely read, a must for all who worship books' *Books and Bookmen*

FUTURA PUBLICATIONS
NON-FICTION
0 8600 7438 2

JOYCE GRENFELL REQUESTS THE PLEASURE

Joyce Grenfell

'Joyce Grenfell has spent three years in compiling a Guide to Joyce Grenfell and her times. This book is the enthralling result. Read, re-read, laugh and cry over this unique book, but *don't* lend it to anyone, because if you do you'll never see it again' *Books and Bookmen*

'The book is full of good stories . . . in her work and in her writing, she achieved the impossible, which is to be both funny and good' *Evening Standard*

'Gripping . . . Joyce Grenfell's brilliant book is a success in the same sense and for the same reasons as were her performances' *The Times*

FUTURA PUBLICATIONS
NON-FICTION/AUTOBIOGRAPHY
0 8600 7571 0

All Futura Books are available at your bookshop or
newsagent, or can be ordered from the following address:
Futura Books, Cash Sales Department,
P.O. Box 11, Falmouth, Cornwall TR10 9EN.

Please send cheque or postal order (no currency), and
allow 60p for postage and packing for the first book
plus 25p for the second book and 15p for each additional
book ordered up to a maximum charge of £1.90 in U.K.

B.F.P.O. customers please allow 60p for
the first book, 25p for the second book plus 15p per
copy for the next 7 books, thereafter 9p per book

Overseas customers, including Eire, please allow £1.25
for postage and packing for the first book, 75p for the
second book and 28p for each subsequent title ordered.